EAST OF EDEN

John Steinbeck

Spark Publishing
A Division of Barnes & Noble
120 Fifth Avenue
New York, NY 10011
www.sparknotes.com

ISBN-13: 978-1-4114-0078-8
ISBN-10: 1-4114-0078-X

Please submit changes or report errors to www.sparknotes.com/errors.

Printed and bound in the United States

7   9   10   8

Introduction:
Stopping to Buy SparkNotes on a Snowy Evening

Whose words these are you *think* you know.
Your paper's due tomorrow, though;
We're glad to see you stopping here
To get some help before you go.

Lost your course? You'll find it here.
Face tests and essays without fear.
Between the words, good grades at stake:
Get great results throughout the year.

Once school bells caused your heart to quake
As teachers circled each mistake.
Use SparkNotes and no longer weep,
Ace every single test you take.

Yes, books are lovely, dark, and deep,
But only what you grasp you keep,
With hours to go before you sleep,
With hours to go before you sleep.

CONTENTS

CONTEXT   1
    BIBLICAL BACKGROUND   2

PLOT OVERVIEW   5

CHARACTER LIST   9
    THE TRASK FAMILY   9
    THE HAMILTON FAMILY   11
    OTHER CHARACTERS   13

ANALYSIS OF MAJOR CHARACTERS   15
    CAL TRASK   15
    ARON TRASK   15
    ADAM TRASK   16
    CATHY AMES   16
    SAMUEL HAMILTON   17

THEMES, MOTIFS, & SYMBOLS   18
    THE PERPETUAL CONTEST BETWEEN GOOD AND EVIL   18
    THE FREEDOM TO OVERCOME EVIL   19
    THE PAIN OF PATERNAL REJECTION   19
    THE STORY OF CAIN AND ABEL   20
    FORTUNES AND INHERITANCES   21
    THE SALINAS VALLEY   21
    CHARLES'S SCAR   22

SUMMARY & ANALYSIS   23
    PART ONE, CHAPTERS 1–5   23
    PART ONE, CHAPTERS 6–11   26
    PART TWO, CHAPTERS 12–17   31
    PART TWO, CHAPTERS 18–22   35
    PART THREE, CHAPTERS 23–26   38
    PART THREE, CHAPTERS 27–33   41
    PART FOUR, CHAPTERS 34–40   45
    PART FOUR, CHAPTERS 41–44   49
    PART FOUR, CHAPTERS 45–50   51
    PART FOUR, CHAPTERS 51–55   55

IMPORTANT QUOTATIONS EXPLAINED   59

KEY FACTS   62

STUDY QUESTIONS & ESSAY TOPICS   65
   STUDY QUESTIONS   65
   SUGGESTED ESSAY TOPICS   68

REVIEW & RESOURCES   69
   QUIZ   69
   SUGGESTIONS FOR FURTHER READING 74

CONTEXT

John Steinbeck is perhaps the quintessential California novelist. Born in Salinas, California, in 1902, he went on to create a body of work that is closely connected to the land, people, and history of his home state. As a young man, Steinbeck worked as a hired hand on farms and ranches throughout the Salinas Valley, forming lasting impressions of the land and its people that would influence virtually all of his later work. Meanwhile, his father, a local government official, and his mother, a former schoolteacher, encouraged his burgeoning interest in writing. After finishing high school, Steinbeck started at Stanford University in Palo Alto but left before finishing his degree in order to pursue work as a reporter in New York City. He returned to California the following year, supporting his writing endeavors with a steady income from manual labor.

The first three novels Steinbeck published—*Cup of Gold* (1929), *The Pastures of Heaven* (1932), and *To a God Unknown* (1933)— were critical and commercial failures. He persisted in his writing, however, and attracted more positive notices with *Tortilla Flat* (1935), a collection of stories about the ethnic working poor in California. *Of Mice and Men* (1937) brought him increased acclaim, and then *The Grapes of Wrath* (1939) earned him widespread fame and the Pulitzer Prize. The story of a family of migrant farmers making the difficult journey from Oklahoma to California during the Great Depression, *The Grapes of Wrath* was hailed as an instant classic and a landmark of socially conscious American fiction.

Steinbeck's novels are acclaimed for their combination of realistic naturalism and moral optimism—two qualities not commonly found together. Steinbeck portrayed the pain, poverty, and wickedness of the world with unsparing detail while at the same time maintained a belief in the "perfectibility of man." This optimism pervades Steinbeck's fiction, leavening even his gloomiest accounts of the Great Depression with a powerful sense of hope.

The sweeping California epic *East of Eden* (1952) is considered Steinbeck's most ambitious work and the masterpiece of his later artistic career. Indeed, although *The Grapes of Wrath* is more famous and widely read, Steinbeck himself regarded *East of Eden* as his greatest novel. He wrote that he believed he had imbued *East of*

Eden with everything he knew about writing and everything he knew about good and evil in the human condition. Though its story is not autobiographical, *East of Eden* does delve into the world of Steinbeck's childhood, incorporating his memories of the Salinas Valley in the early years of the twentieth century, his memories of the war era, and his memories of his relatives, many of whom are secondary characters in the novel. (Samuel Hamilton was indeed Steinbeck's grandfather, Olive Hamilton was Steinbeck's mother, and Aron Trask's gloomy experience at Stanford University is to some degree based on Steinbeck's own unsatisfying years there.)

East of Eden, which was a bestseller upon its publication, cemented Steinbeck's position as one of the most read and beloved American writers of his time. The novel was not, however, a great critical success, as a number of reviewers believed that Steinbeck's epic portrait of the human struggle between good and evil was painted so broadly that it detracted from the detail and believability of his portrayals of individual characters. Despite these mixed critical reviews, Steinbeck continued to write and produced several more works, notably the popular nonfiction piece *Travels with Charley* (1962). For his contributions to twentieth-century fiction, Steinbeck was awarded the Nobel Prize for Literature in 1962. He died in New York City in 1968 and was buried in his hometown of Salinas.

BIBLICAL BACKGROUND

The story of Adam and Eve and the story of their sons, Cain and Abel, form the foundation of the narrative of *East of Eden*. The stories, which appear in Genesis, the first book of the Bible, are the basis of Steinbeck's exploration of the conflict between good and evil in human life.

THE STORY OF ADAM AND EVE
The book of Genesis opens with the story of creation. After creating the world in six days, God declares his intention to make a being in his own image. He then creates humankind. God fashions a man out of dust and names him Adam. Then, God forms a woman out of Adam's rib, and Adam names her Eve. God places Adam and Eve on Earth in the idyllic garden of Eden. He encourages them to procreate and to enjoy the created world fully but forbids them to eat from the tree of the knowledge of good and evil, which grows in the garden.

One day in the garden, Satan approaches Eve in the form of a crafty serpent. He convinces her to eat the tree's forbidden fruit, assuring her that she will not suffer if she does so. Eve eats from the tree and then shares the fruit with Adam, and the two immediately are filled with shame and remorse. God discovers Adam and Eve's disobedience. In punishment, God curses Eve to suffer painful childbirth and to submit to her husband's authority; he curses Adam to toil and work the ground for food. God then banishes Adam and Eve from Eden.

THE STORY OF CAIN AND ABEL

Sent out into the world, Adam and Eve give birth to two sons, Cain and Abel. Cain becomes a farmer, Abel a shepherd. One day, the two brothers bring sacrifices to God. Cain offers God grain from his fields, while Abel offers the fattest portion of his flocks. For an unknown reason, God favors Abel's offering over Cain's. Cain, out of jealousy, murders Abel. When God sees that Abel is missing and asks Cain where Abel is, Cain retorts, "Am I my brother's keeper?"

God realizes that Abel is dead and punishes Cain by condemning him to exile. When Cain protests that the punishment is too severe and will put his life in danger, God puts a mark on Cain to warn others not to harm or kill him, for if they do so, they will be punished sevenfold. God then banishes Cain from his home to wander in the land of Nod, which lies to the east of Eden.

Plot Overview

I n the late nineteenth century, a man named Samuel Hamilton settles in the Salinas Valley in northern California. He brings his strict but loving wife, Liza, with him from Ireland. Although Samuel is well respected in the community, he never becomes a wealthy man. The Hamiltons go on to have nine children and become a prominent family in the valley.

Adam Trask, meanwhile, settles in the valley with his pregnant wife Cathy where he eventually becomes friends with Samuel Hamilton. Before moving to California, Adam lives on a farm in Connecticut with his half-brother, Charles. The dark and moody Charles resents the fact that his and Adam's father, Cyrus, has always favored the good-natured Adam. Upon his death, Cyrus leaves his sons a large and unexpected fortune, probably stolen during his days as an administrator in the U.S. Army. Despite their new-found wealth, Adam and Charles remain unable to get along. Charles is disgusted at his brother's marriage to Cathy, who, unbeknownst to Adam or Charles, is a former prostitute who murdered her parents and stole their money. Although Charles despises Cathy, he takes her into his bed after she drugs Adam on their wedding night.

Adam and Cathy move to California, as Adam proves unable to live peacefully with Charles in Connecticut. In Salinas, Cathy learns she is pregnant and attempts to abort her baby in order to prevent any furtherance of ties to her husband. She is desperate to escape Adam despite the fact that he loves her and provides for her. The abortion is unsuccessful, and Cathy eventually gives birth to twins, Aron and Caleb (Cal). It is clear from the start, however, that Cathy does not care about the infants and wants to leave the household as soon as possible. One day, Cathy shoots Adam, flees the house, and moves to Salinas proper to resume her life as a prostitute. Adam decides to cover for Cathy by lying to the local sheriff and saying that his gunshot wound was an accident.

Cathy wins the trust of Faye, the madam of a local brothel, then poisons her and fools the doctors and other prostitutes into thinking that Faye died naturally. Cathy assumes control of the brothel and starts to blackmail powerful men in Salinas with photographs of them performing sadomasochistic sex acts with her and her prostitutes. To protect the dazed Adam and his twin boys, neither Samuel

5

Hamilton nor Lee, Adam's housekeeper, tells Adam or the boys that Cathy works at a brothel.

As the twins grow older, Aron manifests his father's good heart, whereas Cal exhibits his mother's ruthlessness and tendency to manipulate. By the time they reach early adolescence, however, Cal actively struggles against his dark side and prays to God to make him more like Aron. Adam, meanwhile, remains melancholy and listless for years after Cathy's departure. In order to jolt Adam out of his despondency, Samuel finally tells him the truth about Cathy. Samuel dies soon afterward.

After Samuel's funeral, Adam visits Cathy at the brothel. Her deteriorating body and cynical, vulgar talk make Adam realize that he can now move on and forget her, as she is a repugnant creature who has become irrelevant to his life. Cathy, however, is desperate to retain power over Adam. She even offers to have sex with him to keep him in the brothel and prove that he is no better than she. Adam refuses and leaves with a serene smile.

After his triumph over Cathy, Adam becomes a livelier and more committed father to his boys. Adam decides to move the family off the ranch and into the town of Salinas so that Aron and Cal can attend school. The twins are assigned to the seventh grade, and Aron begins a relationship with Abra, the goodhearted daughter of a corrupt county supervisor. Cal continues to struggle with his dark side, and when he finally happens to discover the truth about his mother, he believes that her evil has been passed down to him. But Adam's housekeeper, Lee, who has extensively researched the biblical story of Cain and Abel, advises Cal that God intends each individual to choose his own moral destiny rather than be constrained by the legacy of his parents. This idea, encapsulated by the Hebrew word *timshel* (meaning "thou mayest"), counters Cal's fatalistic idea that he has inherited his mother's evil and sin.

Aron gradually withdraws into religious fervor in order to shield himself from the corruption of the world—an approach that Abra and Lee consider cowardly. Adam, meanwhile, squanders the family fortune on a poorly executed business venture involving refrigerated shipping of vegetables. Aron graduates from high school early and leaves for Stanford University. Adam misses Aron terribly, thinking him smarter and more ambitious than Cal.

However, Cal, in collaboration with Will Hamilton, one of Samuel's sons, works secretly to earn back the fortune his father lost on the failed refrigeration business. Cal also hopes to make enough money to pay for Aron's tuition at Stanford. In the strained economy of World War I, Will and Cal buy beans from local farmers at an unfairly low price and sell the beans, in turn, to desperate British buyers at an unfairly high price. The venture nets Cal thousands of dollars, which he plans to give to his father as a gift at Thanksgiving.

Aron, who is miserable at Stanford, comes home for Thanksgiving. Adam is thrilled to see Aron but appalled by Cal's gift of money. Adam considers the money to be earned dishonestly and tells Cal to give it back to the farmers from whom he stole it. Enraged and jealous of Adam's obvious preference for Aron, Cal loses control of his anger and rashly tells Aron the truth about their mother, Cathy. When Cal takes Aron to the brothel to show him that Cathy is still alive, the revelation crushes the fragile Aron, who screams incoherently and runs away. The next day, the shattered Aron joins the Army, while Cathy, horrified by her son's reaction to her, commits suicide by overdosing on morphine. She leaves her entire fortune—part of it inherited from Charles, part of it earned through blackmail and prostitution—to Aron.

When Adam discovers that Aron has joined the Army, he lapses into a state of shock. Lee talks to Cal about the idea of *timshel* and urges Cal to remember that, despite his guilt, he is a normal, flawed human being—not an aberrant embodiment of evil. This discussion makes Cal feel somewhat better, and he is able to begin a relationship with Abra, who is no longer in love with Aron.

A telegram arrives informing the family that Aron has been killed in World War I. Adam has a severe stroke upon hearing the news, and Lee brings Abra and Cal to see Adam on his deathbed. Lee informs Adam that the guilt-stricken Cal told Aron about their mother only because Cal was convinced that their father loved Aron more than him. Lee asks Adam to offer his blessing to Cal before he dies. At this, Adam raises his hand and whispers the single word *timshel*.

CHARACTER LIST

THE TRASK FAMILY

Cyrus Trask The patriarch of the Trask family and the father of
  Adam and Charles. The imposing Cyrus lies so
  convincingly about his military heroics during the Civil
  War that the government appoints him to a powerful
  position in the Army administration. In fact, Cyrus was
  wounded in the very first hour of his battlefield
  experience in the Civil War and lost his leg to
  amputation. Cyrus leaves his (probably stolen) fortune
  of more than $100,000 to his sons.

Mrs. Trask The first wife of Cyrus Trask and the mother of Adam.
  Cyrus's wife, whose name we do not learn, is a deeply
  pious woman. She contracts syphilis from Cyrus after
  he sleeps with a black prostitute in the South during the
  Civil War. Mrs. Trask commits suicide shortly
  thereafter.

Alice Trask Cyrus's second wife and the mother of Charles. Alice
  is a quiet, deferential woman who almost never shows
  emotion. One day, however, Adam catches her smiling
  mysteriously to herself when she thinks no one is
  watching. Alice dies while Adam is away in the Army,
  fighting Indian tribes in the west.

Adam Trask The son of Cyrus Trask and the father of Aron and
  Cal. Adam is a goodhearted but somewhat impractical
  man, and his innocence leads him to fall in love with
  the novel's most evil character, Cathy Ames. In the
  novel's retelling of the biblical story of Cain and Abel,
  Adam plays the Abel role in the first generation of the
  Trask family; in the second generation, he plays the

9

Adam role befitting his name. Adam's benediction to Cal at the end of the novel validates *timshel,* the idea that individuals are free to choose their own moral paths.

Charles Trask The son of Cyrus Trask and the half-brother of Adam. Charles is a violent, cynical, manipulative man who works his father's farm and greedily amasses a large fortune. Although Charles is deeply jealous of his brother, he also needs Adam and misses him terribly when he is not at home. Charles plays the Cain role in the first generation of the Trasks. He is one of the only characters capable of inspiring fear in the thoroughly evil Cathy Ames.

Aron Trask The son of Adam and Cathy and the twin brother of Cal. Aron is a goodhearted, trusting boy whose deep, innate morality makes it painful for him to hear about or witness evil. As a result, Aron weakens and increasingly retreats into the church as a protection from the harsh realities of the world. Aron plays the Abel role in the second generation of the Trask family. When Cal (the corresponding Cain) reveals to Aron that their mother, Cathy, is a prostitute, Aron is so devastated that he leaves Stanford and joins the army, and soon dies in World War I.

Caleb Trask The son of Adam and Cathy and the twin brother of Aron. Cal is a manipulative, tempestuous boy who is fiercely jealous of his more likable brother, Aron. Cal struggles throughout the second half of the novel to control his temptations and to lead a moral life. Ultimately, he accepts the idea of *timshel,* that every individual is free to choose his own moral path in life. This acceptance enables Cal to overcome his fear that his mother's evil has been passed down to him. At the end of the novel, Cal is the character who most directly embodies this central idea of *timshel.* Cal plays the Cain role in the second generation of the Trask family, indirectly killing Aron (the corresponding Abel) by revealing to Aron that their mother is a prostitute, which leads Aron to join the army and die in World War I. When his father confronts him about Aron's whereabouts, Cal sneers, "Am I supposed to look after him?"—an echo of Cain's famous retort to God, "Am I my brother's keeper?"

THE HAMILTON FAMILY

Samuel Hamilton The patriarch of the Hamilton family. Samuel is a joyous, self-educated Irishman who moves his family to the Salinas Valley in California. Although he is never a rich man, he is well respected in the community. Against the wishes of his wife, Liza, Samuel befriends Adam Trask. Samuel remains a youthful, vigorous man until the death of his daughter Una, which hurts him deeply.

Liza Hamilton Samuel's wife and the mother of their nine children. The tiny Liza is a strict, moral woman who loves her husband and her family very much. The narrator marvels at Liza's ability to have so many children, feed them, make their clothes, and instill "good manners and iron morals" in them all at the same time.

George Hamilton The eldest son of Samuel and Liza. George, who is a very minor character in the novel, is bland but has an aura of courtliness about him.

Will Hamilton The second son of Samuel and Liza. The practical and conservative Will has a Midas touch in business dealings. He becomes wealthy and powerful in the Salinas community, but his business success alienates him from his family somewhat.

Tom Hamilton The third son of Samuel and Liza. Tom is ardent and passionate, in stark contrast to his brother Will. After Tom indirectly causes the death of his sister Dessie by giving her stomach-soothing salts that aggravate her severe illness, he kills himself out of guilt and grief.

Joe Hamilton The youngest son of Samuel and Liza. Joe, a dreamer and academic by nature, attends Stanford University and then moves to the east, where he has great success in the emerging field of advertising.

Lizzie Hamilton The eldest daughter of Samuel and Liza. Lizzie, a very minor character, essentially leaves the Hamilton family and chooses instead to associate herself with her husband's family. She has a capacity for hatred and bitterness that the rest of the Hamiltons do not share.

Una Hamilton The second daughter of Samuel and Liza. The dark and brooding Una marries, moves with her husband to a remote area on the Oregon border, and dies not long after the move. Her death crushes Samuel and ages him considerably.

Dessie Hamilton The third daughter of Samuel and Liza. Dessie, who runs a dressmaking shop in Salinas, is not beautiful but has a lovely personality that makes everyone enjoy her company. She dies when Tom gives her salts to soothe her stomach, accidentally aggravating her illness.

Olive Hamilton The fourth daughter of Samuel and Liza. Olive becomes a teacher, which makes her family proud. She is the mother of the narrator of the novel (and indeed, in real life, the mother of John Steinbeck).

Mollie Hamilton The youngest daughter of Samuel and Liza. Mollie is the lovely one, the sweetheart of the family. She marries and moves to an apartment in San Francisco.

OTHER CHARACTERS

Cathy Ames A moral monster, the most evil character in the novel. Cathy acts out of a perverse love of debasement, destruction, and control. As a young girl, she murders her parents by arson and then commences a life of prostitution. She later marries and then shoots Adam Trask, abandoning her newborn twin sons in order to return to prostitution. After murdering the brothel owner, Faye, Cathy becomes the madam of the brothel, using drugs to control and manipulate her whores. She takes photographs of powerful men involved in sadomasochistic sex acts in order to blackmail them. Aron's discovery that Cathy is his mother shatters him and spurs the chain of events that leads to his death. Cathy represents Eve in the Cain and Abel story of the novel, introducing sin and evil into the world. She commits suicide after enduring Aron's response to her. (For the sake of consistency, this SparkNote refers to her as Cathy throughout, though at various points in the novel she goes by the name Catherine or Kate as she attempts to cover her identity.)

Lee Adam Trask's dutiful cook and housekeeper, an educated man whose parents emigrated to America from China. Lee often affects a Chinese pidgin accent to play into Americans' expectations of him. A philosophical man, he frequently gives voice to the novel's themes, including the crucial idea of *timshel*. Throughout the novel, Lee serves as a stabilizing force in the Trask household.

Abra Bacon The daughter of the corrupt county supervisor in Salinas. Abra, who is as goodhearted as Cathy is evil, offers compassion and common sense to the tumultuous Trask family. Abra falls in love with Aron, but after his cowardly withdrawal into the church, she shifts her affections to Cal. Like Cal, Abra worries that her father's corruption—the narrator implies that he steals money and that he is one of the men whom Cathy blackmails—will taint her. However, with Cal, Abra learns the lesson of *timshel*—that she is free to choose her own moral destiny.

Mr. Edwards   A man who runs a prostitution ring throughout Massachusetts and Connecticut. Mr. Edwards has a highly moral wife and a pair of sons who attend the prestigious Groton School, and he leads a largely respectable life despite his base profession. After employing Cathy as a prostitute, Mr. Edwards falls in love with her. Upon discovering her involvement in the murder of her parents, he beats her nearly to death, and she crawls away to the nearest farm—that owned by Charles and Adam Trask.

Faye   The madam at the Salinas whorehouse where Cathy works as a prostitute. Cathy poisons Faye gradually, and after Faye finally dies, takes over the brothel.

Ethel   A prostitute at Faye's brothel who obtains proof that Cathy murdered Faye. Ethel tries to blackmail Cathy for a payment of $100 each month but is later discovered to have drowned.

Joe Valery   An escaped convict who is employed as a bouncer at Cathy's brothel. As Cathy degenerates, Joe assumes increasing influence and control over her brothel. Before Cathy kills herself, she informs the police about Joe's earlier jailbreak. Just as Joe is about to leave town with Cathy's money, he is found and gunned down by a deputy as he tries to escape.

ANALYSIS OF MAJOR CHARACTERS

CAL TRASK

Cal is perhaps the most complex character in *East of Eden* and the one who embodies the concept of *timshel* most directly. Whereas Adam is the protagonist of the early parts of novel, the focus shifts to Cal in the later chapters. At first, it appears that Cal has inherited the evil tendencies of his mother, Cathy, and that he is destined to fulfill the role of Cain in his generation. Indeed, Cal does display the characteristics of a Cain figure: he becomes fiercely jealous of Aron because of Adam's obvious preference for him, and ultimately sets in motion the events that lead to Aron's death, even uttering a parallel of the biblical Cain's retort to God about being his "brother's keeper." Although Cal is seemingly "born" into an evil path, he struggles against what he sees as his inherited evil—the evil of his mother, Cathy—and prays to God to put him on the path toward good. Although Cal does make several poor moral choices as he is growing up, he ultimately takes Lee's advice and recognizes the validity of *timshel*, the idea that each individual has the power to choose between good and evil in life. Thus, while Cal is indeed a Cain figure, he demonstrates the ability to break out of inherited sin and act for good instead.

ARON TRASK

Aron, as the Abel figure of his generation, is goodhearted and trusting like his father, Adam. Although Aron is likable and kind, his innate moral sensitivity is extreme, and it makes him fragile and easily susceptible to hurt. The sheltered Aron has a great deal of trouble facing the reality of human evil in the world, and Steinbeck builds a great deal of suspense in the second half of *East of Eden* regarding whether or not Aron will ever meet his mother, Cathy, and whether or not he will survive such an encounter. Gradually, Aron retreats into the shelter of the church, rejecting the love of Abra in favor of religious laws of chastity and devotion. For a time, Aron also uses higher education as an escape, as he flees to Stanford University but then returns home a short time later, miserable. As the second half of the novel progresses, Aron becomes less likable, as we sense that the shelters he seeks are hollow and that his pursuits are driven neither by true religious belief nor a desire for intellectual education. Ultimately, Aron is destroyed by the revelation that Cathy is his mother. He retreats into a final escape—enlistment in the army—and is killed in World War I. Aron's death is foreshadowed not only by his role as an Abel figure, but also by Samuel Hamilton's musing that Aron's namesake, the biblical Aaron, did not make it to the Promised Land of Canaan.

ADAM TRASK

The protagonist of the first half of the novel, Adam is a kind but flawed man who makes a number of bad decisions at crucial points of the story. Adam's biggest flaws are his tendency to be too trusting and his failure to see people for who they really are. It is these characteristics that make him blind to his father's corruption and to Cathy's, scheming and manipulation. Adam's trusting and good-hearted nature sets him up as an Abel figure in the first generation of the Trask family, as he is his father's favorite and inadvertently incites the jealousy of his brother, Charles. As Adam grows older and has his own sons, his symbolic role changes and he becomes a parallel to the biblical Adam, Cain and Abel's father. For much of the boys' childhood, Adam proves a less than ideal father, distant from his sons and unable to see his own favoritism for Aron over Cal—a repetition of his own father's favoritism, which proves damaging to the family once again. Adam lavishes all of his love and attention on the anemic and aloof Aron while largely writing off the more loving and thoughtful Cal. Ultimately, however, Lee causes Adam to realize Cal's potential, and Adam redeems Cal by blessing him at the end of the novel.

CATHY AMES

The parasitic, manipulative Cathy is the embodiment of evil in the novel and the most static of the main characters. Her evil seems to be innate and all-consuming, as she displays murderous and sexually perverse tendencies from an early age. A figure of infertility and destruction who kills her parents and attempts to kill her own unborn children, Cathy is a debased version of the biblical Eve, whom the Christian tradition sees as the mother of all humankind. Like Eve, Cathy is associated with sin, but whereas Eve is deceived into committing sin, Cathy embraces it wholeheartedly and commits evil simply for its own sake. Cathy has an overwhelmingly pessimistic view of humankind: she believes that there is only evil in the world and therefore surrenders herself to it fully. All the while, she fails to understand the good in other characters and instead uses their trusting natures to achieve her own predatory ends. Notably, we never get any sense that Cathy is using her evil acts to reach any sort of ultimate goal or aim. For this reason, some critics have dismissed Cathy as an implausible character and a major weak link in Steinbeck's novel. The narrator of *East of Eden* himself is somewhat confounded by Cathy, as he struggles to understand her and revises his opinion of her throughout the novel. In any case, Cathy is a symbol of the human evil that will always be present in the world, and her loss of power over Adam and Cal bolsters the novel's message that individuals have the choice to reject evil in favor of good.

SAMUEL HAMILTON

As the gentle, selfless patriarch of the Hamilton family, Samuel stands in sharp contrast to Cyrus, the dishonest patriarch of the Trask family. Whereas Cyrus introduces a legacy of sin into his family by passing down a stolen inheritance, the good-natured Samuel—who, notably, never is wealthy—passes down an inheritance of close familial love and devotion. Like the biblical Samuel, who was a prophet, Samuel Hamilton displays intuition and foresight and often tells Adam Trask truths that are difficult to hear. Samuel sees through Cathy immediately and is chilled by her inhumanity and Adam's ignorance of it. After the twins are born and Cathy flees, Samuel counsels Adam and helps him overcome his melancholy. Although Samuel is not a violent man, he reluctantly resorts to force in order to jolt Adam out of his stupor and to convince Adam to give the boys names, which they go without for more than a year. Later, shortly before he dies of old age, Samuel tells Adam the difficult truth that Cathy is still living in Salinas and working at a brothel. Although this revelation causes Adam pain, it ultimately enables him to confront the reality of Cathy's evil and escape from her power.

THEMES, MOTIFS, & SYMBOLS

THEMES

Themes are the fundamental and often universal ideas explored in a literary work.

THE PERPETUAL CONTEST BETWEEN GOOD AND EVIL

In Chapter 34 of *East of Eden*, the narrator articulates his belief that the struggle between good and evil is the one recurring narrative of human history. In fact, he goes so far as to state that there "is no other story." Writing from the perspective of the Christian tradition, the narrator contends that every human individual since Adam and Eve and Cain and Abel has struggled with the choice between good and evil. The narrator writes that each person, when looking back on his or her life, "will have left only the hard, clean questions: Was it good or was it evil? Have I done well—or ill?" Because the struggle is an individual one, the narrator implies that no progress is made through the generations—each person must reenact the same ancient story and grapple with the same ancient problems.

East of Eden dramatizes this perpetual conflict between good and evil in the society of the Salinas Valley as a whole and within the individuals of the Trask and Hamilton families in particular. The main characters of the novel, generation after generation, wrestle with the problem of evil. Cyrus, the patriarch of the Trask family, apparently chooses evil by stealing money during his term as a U.S. Army administrator. Charles succumbs to jealousy of his brother, Adam. Cathy takes the path of evil at every turn, manipulating and wounding others for her own benefit. Cal, worried that he has inherited a legacy of sin from his mother, struggles perhaps the hardest of all the characters. Ultimately, the novel ends on a positive note, as Cal accepts the possibility and responsibility of free will—of free choice between good and evil. This optimistic ending is tempered, however, by our knowledge that future generations will endlessly replay the same struggle that Cal and his ancestors have endured.

THE FREEDOM TO OVERCOME EVIL

Although one of the fundamental ideas in *East of Eden* is that evil is an innate and inescapable human problem, the novel also sets forth hope that each individual has the freedom to overcome evil by his or her own choice. This idea of free choice is encapsulated in the Hebrew word *timshel,* the meaning of which Adam's housekeeper, Lee, has researched. The word, which translates to "thou mayest," appears in the story of Cain and Abel in the Bible, when God tells Cain that he has the freedom to *choose* to overcome sin. Lee sees this idea of free will as central to the human condition—in fact, he says that *timshel* might be the "most important word in the world."

The other characters in *East of Eden* have different opinions regarding whether or not individuals can truly overcome evil by free choice. Cathy, for instance, insists that there is only evil in the world, so she immerses herself in it and exploits other people's human weaknesses to her own advantage. Aron, meanwhile, is only able to face the good in the world, and the evil that his mother embodies ultimately proves too much for him to handle. Cal struggles to find a middle road between these two extremes. Ultimately, he is successful, as he accepts Lee's belief that evil can be overcome and that morality is a free choice, regardless of the fact that all humans are imperfect, sinful beings. With this newfound knowledge, Cal is able to go forward into a new life with Abra, confident that he controls his own moral destiny.

THE PAIN OF PATERNAL REJECTION

The dynamics of father-son relationships, especially the issue of a father's preference for one son over another, are central to the story told in *East of Eden.* In the first generation of the Trask family covered in the novel, Cyrus displays a clear preference for Adam over Charles, for no discernible reason. Charles, who seems to love his father far more than Adam does, senses this disapproval from his father and resents it deeply. Charles's resentment comes to a head when Cyrus prefers the birthday gift Adam gives him (a stray puppy, to which Adam gives hardly any thought) to the gift Charles gives him (a knife for which Charles works hard to save money in order to buy). Once again, Cyrus's preference for the puppy over the knife appears to be completely arbitrary, and the disapproval enrages Charles. Later, Adam displays the same kind of arbitrary favoritism in his relationships with his own sons, Aron and Cal. Aron grows up to be somewhat cowardly and fragile, while Cal courageously strug-

THEMES

gles to stay on the path of good amid numerous temptations toward evil. Nonetheless, Adam perceives Aron as ambitious and promising but dismisses Cal as shiftless and directionless.

Steinbeck patterns these father-son relationships in the Trask family on an example in the Bible—the relationships that the brothers Cain and Abel have with God, who represents a father figure to both of them. When Cain and Abel both offer sacrifices to God (mirrored in Steinbeck's novel by Charles's and Adam's birthday gifts to Cyrus), God favors Abel's sacrifice over Cain's. Conspicuously, neither God nor the narrator of the story in the Bible offers any reason or justification for God's preference. In *East of Eden,* Adam mentions that, upon reading the story of Cain and Abel, he felt "a little outraged at God" for favoring Abel so arbitrarily. However, as we see, Adam favors Aron over Cal just as arbitrarily as God favors Abel over Cain. Adam does not realize the depth of his favoritism until he is on his deathbed, when he acknowledges the mistake he has made and grants his final blessing to Cal.

MOTIFS

Motifs are recurring structures, contrasts, or literary devices that can help to develop and inform the text's major themes.

THE STORY OF CAIN AND ABEL

Throughout the course of *East of Eden,* different members of the Trask family correspond to the biblical Cain and Abel at different times. In the first Trask generation, Charles and Adam correspond to Cain and Abel, respectively. Like the biblical Cain, Charles grows jealous of his brother, Adam, and attacks him in rage—Charles does not, however, cause his brother's death. As the novel progresses, Adam relinquishes his role as an Abel figure and takes on the role of his biblical namesake, Adam, the first human. Adam's sons, Cal and Aron, become the respective parallels to Cain and Abel in the new generation of the Trask family. Again, Cal, the Cain figure, becomes jealous of his brother, Aron. In this iteration of the story, Cal's hurtful actions indirectly cause Aron's enlistment in the army and subsequent death in World War I. When Adam asks Cal where Aron has gone, Cal sneers, "Am I supposed to look out for him?"—a parallel to Cain's famous retort to God after murdering Abel, "Am I my brother's keeper?" In indirectly causing Aron's death, Cal succumbs, like Cain, to his evil instincts. However, unlike Cain, Cal ultimately understands that he has free will to overcome sin and, on the final page of the novel, is redeemed by his father's blessing.

FORTUNES AND INHERITANCES

The Trask family fortune is an emblem of the idea of original sin—the sin that, by the Christian tradition, has been passed down through every human generation since the fall of the biblical Adam and Eve. In *East of Eden,* Cyrus leaves his fortune, likely earned through corruption, to Charles and Adam. When Charles dies, he passes on his share to Adam and Cathy. Adam subsequently squanders his share on a failed business venture, while Cathy increases it through her work at the brothel and then passes it on solely to Aron. In blowing the inheritance on his failed business, Adam essentially sidesteps its moral taint. Aron, however, is forced to bear the full burden of it himself. This symbolic burden of sin proves too much for Adam and ultimately leads to his death. Cal, meanwhile, is left out of the Trask inheritance and escapes untainted. Through this turn of events, Cal avoids his family's legacy of sin and evil and realizes he has the freedom to choose his own moral path.

SYMBOLS

Symbols are objects, characters, figures, or colors used to represent abstract ideas or concepts.

THE SALINAS VALLEY

Although the Salinas Valley in northern California provides the setting for several of Steinbeck's works, its role is arguably greatest in *East of Eden.* In fact, *The Salinas Valley* was one of Steinbeck's working titles for the novel, which Steinbeck described as "a sort of autobiography of the Salinas Valley." The narrator opens *East of Eden* with a nostalgic, lyrical description of the valley, recalling the sights, smells, and other memories of his Salinas childhood. He also establishes the valley as a symbolic arena for the struggle between good and evil: the valley is enclosed by the inviting Gabilan Mountains to the east—"light gay mountains full of sun and loveliness"—and the "dark and brooding" Santa Lucia Mountains to the west. Described in such a manner, the mountains symbolize the human struggle to navigate between good and evil. The Salinas Valley between them can be seen as a representation of the lands where the biblical Adam and Eve live after God banishes them from Eden.

After being driven from Eden, Adam and Eve are forced to live in a world in which the dangers and temptations of evil are ever-present. Likewise, the main characters in *East of Eden* struggle to exercise free will in the face of the inherited evils of their ancestors.

CHARLES'S SCAR

Early in the novel, Charles Trask loses his temper while struggling to move a large boulder from his yard and, in the process, cuts his forehead badly with the crowbar he is using to pry out the rock. The wound heals but leaves a large, ugly scar that, unlike most scars, is darker than the skin that surrounds it. Charles's scar corresponds to the "mark of Cain" in the biblical story of Cain and Abel. After God discovers Cain's murder of Abel, he banishes Cain to the lands east of Eden and puts a mark on Cain so that no one who encounters him will kill him. In this regard, the mark is not a curse but a form of protection. In *East of Eden,* Charles's own words highlight this symbolic connection. In a letter to his brother, Adam, Charles writes about the scar: "I don't know why it bothers me. I got plenty other scars. It just seems like I was marked." Charles's words make the symbolic connection unmistakable and reinforce the relationship between Charles and Adam as a surrogate for the relationship between Cain and Abel—a relationship that Cal and Aron repeat in the next generation.

SUMMARY & ANALYSIS

PART ONE, CHAPTERS 1–5

SUMMARY: CHAPTER 1
The narrator begins by describing his childhood in California's Salinas Valley, where he learned to tell east from west by looking at the mountains—the bright Gabilan Mountains to the east and the dark Santa Lucia Mountains to the west. The valley's weather comes in thirty-year cycles: five or six years of heavy rainfall, six or seven years of moderate rainfall, and then many years of dryness. The valley was settled by three peoples: first, the Indians, whom the narrator derides as lazy; next, the Spanish, whom the narrator calls greedy; and finally, the Americans, who the narrator says are even greedier than the Spanish.

SUMMARY: CHAPTER 2
In 1870, Samuel and Liza Hamilton—the narrator's grandparents—arrive in the Salinas Valley from Ireland. The Hamiltons are forced to settle on the driest and most barren land in the valley, as all the better lots are already taken. To support his nine children, Samuel works as a blacksmith, a well-digger, and an unlicensed doctor.

SUMMARY: CHAPTER 3
Some time after Samuel Hamilton arrives, a man named Adam Trask settles a fertile corner of the Salinas Valley for himself and lives as a wealthy man. After introducing Adam, the narrator jumps back in time to tell the story of Adam's childhood.

Adam is the son of Cyrus Trask, a conniving Connecticut farmer who loses a leg in the Civil War and then passes on syphilis to his wife after contracting it from a black prostitute in the South. Cyrus's pious wife commits suicide shortly after discovering her illness. Cyrus needs help with the children, so he marries a young woman named Alice, who lives in fear of her husband and even hides her tuberculosis from him out of worry that he might impose a harsh medical treatment upon her. In his spare time, Cyrus studies military history and strategy so that he might create convincing lies about his time in the Army. His lies about his alleged heroics in the Civil War gain him widespread respect and ultimately an appointment as Secretary of the Army.

As a boy, Adam Trask is kind and good-natured, but his half-brother, Charles, is boisterous and aggressive. One day, Charles beats Adam severely simply because Adam defeats him in a game. Adam loves his stepmother, Alice, and anonymously leaves her secret gifts in order to make her smile.

When Adam is a young man, Cyrus tries to convince him to go into the Army. When Adam asks his father why he does not want Charles to go into the army instead, Cyrus responds that the army would cultivate a part of Charles's nature that needs to be suppressed. In addition, Cyrus says that he loves Adam better.

Later, Charles asks Adam about his conversation with their father. Adam learns that Charles is resentful about Cyrus's recent birthday: Cyrus was completely indifferent to the expensive German knife Charles gave him as a gift, yet deeply appreciated the stray puppy Adam gave him. Suddenly, the jealous Charles beats Adam severely and leaves him in a ditch on the side of the road.

Adam limps home much later and weakly tells Cyrus that Charles thinks Cyrus does not love him. Cyrus leaves with a shotgun in search of Charles. Alice tends to Adam and tells him that Charles has a kind streak as well. It turns out that Alice mistakenly believes that Charles, not Adam, is the one who has been leaving her secret gifts for years.

SUMMARY: CHAPTER 4
Charles wisely stays away from home for two weeks. When he returns, Cyrus is over his rage and puts him to work.

SUMMARY: CHAPTER 5
Samuel Hamilton educated himself in Ireland by borrowing books from a wealthy family. In America, his gentle good nature wins him the respect of everyone he meets. The Hamiltons never become rich but live comfortably nonetheless. They have four sons: George, who is bland and moral; Will, who is lucky and grows up to be wealthy; Tom, who is ardent and passionate; and Joe, who is lazy but likable and intelligent. Samuel and Liza also have five daughters: Lizzie, who does not associate with the family very much; Una, who is dark and brooding; Dessie, whose lovely personality makes her well-loved; Olive, the narrator's mother, who becomes a teacher; and Mollie, the baby and beauty of the family.

Liza Hamilton, like her husband, is highly respected in the Salinas valley. She strictly disapproves of alcoholic beverages until the age of seventy, when her doctor tells her to take port wine for medical reasons. From that day forward, the old woman drinks lustily.

ANALYSIS: CHAPTERS 1–5

The central concern of *East of Eden* is the struggle between good and evil within individuals and in society as a whole, and Steinbeck explores this struggle through a number of sets of contrasts. He opens the novel with a description of the Salinas Valley where he grew up, establishing an important early metaphor for the conflict between good and evil—the contrast between the dark, foreboding Santa Lucia Mountains to the west and the bright, welcoming Gabilan Mountains to the east. The narrator, whose voice is essentially that of Steinbeck, says that he learned to tell east from west by looking at these mountains. This role of the mountains symbolizes the human predicament of having to navigate between light and darkness, goodness and evil. Additionally, the opening chapters reveal the narrator's tendency to meditate on history in violent and dramatic terms. In the opening chapter, we see that he tends to view the events of the past as inspired by greed and brutality. Later in the novel, he says that there is "only one story in the world"—the human struggle between good and evil.

Perhaps the most important contrast explored in this first section is that between the large, loving Hamilton family and the small, tension-ridden Trask family. In his portrayals of the patriarchs of these two families—Samuel Hamilton and Cyrus Trask, respectively—Steinbeck quickly establishes the different moral environments in which the children of the two families later develop. Samuel Hamilton is a powerful force of good and familial strength throughout the novel, whereas Cyrus Trask is a menacing figure of corruption and familial divisiveness. This initial contrast between the heads of the two families persists in the subsequent generations, as the Hamiltons remain close and loving while the Trasks are fraught with strife and hostility. We see this strife played out immediately in the next generation of the Trask family, as the good-natured and kind Adam frequently comes into conflict with the violent and manipulative Charles.

The biblical story of Cain and Abel, the sons of Adam and Eve, provides the basic template for many of the relationships in *East of Eden*—in the early parts of the novel, the relationship between.

Charles and Adam. According to the Bible, Cain is a farmer, Abel a shepherd. When the two brothers bring sacrifices to God one day, Cain offers grain from his fields, while Abel offers the fattest portion of his flocks. God, seemingly arbitrarily, favors Abel's offering over Cain's. Cain then murders Abel out of jealousy. As punishment, God banishes Cain to the land of Nod, which lies "on the east of Eden"—hence the title of Steinbeck's novel. In *East of Eden,* Charles and Adam mirror this biblical gift-giving in their birthday gifts to their father, Cyrus. Charles diligently saves money to buy Cyrus a German knife, while Adam, who hardly gives the gift a thought, presents Cyrus with a stray puppy he has found. Cyrus far prefers Adam's gift to Charles's, favors Adam in general, and even admits that he loves Adam more. Like Cain, Charles becomes intensely jealous and takes out his frustration on Adam, beating him brutally. But Charles, unlike Cain, does not kill his brother; for the moment, evil (Cain/Charles) and good (Abel/Adam) are locked in a struggle in which it seems that evil has the upper hand.

PART ONE, CHAPTERS 6–11

SUMMARY: CHAPTER 6

Young Adam Trask joins his Army regiment around the same time that Cyrus moves to Washington to become a Secretary of the Army. Charles takes over the job of running the Trask farm in Connecticut, living alone and visiting prostitutes twice a month. One day, Charles cuts his forehead badly while moving a large boulder from his yard. Ultimately, he develops an ugly, dark scar on his face. Ashamed of his disfigurement, Charles visits the town even less often and longs for Adam's return.

Adam is discharged from the Army in 1885 but soon realizes that he misses life in the Army and decides to enlist again. He is sent to Washington, where he encounters Cyrus, now dressed in fine clothing and fitted with a fancy prosthetic leg. Cyrus tells Adam that he could get Adam into the military academy at West Point, but Adam insists that he just wants to go back to his old regiment. Charles is crushed when Adam does not return to the farm. After a year and several letters, Adam succeeds in reestablishing contact with his brother. The two never have much in common, however, which makes their relationship difficult.

SUMMARY: CHAPTER 7

After five years fighting in campaigns against Native Americans in the west, Adam again is discharged from the Army. As he slowly makes his way across the country back to the farm in Connecticut, he slips into a life as a drifter and is eventually arrested for vagrancy and placed on a chain gang. In February 1894, Cyrus dies and leaves a large fortune—more than $100,000—to his sons, who are to split it evenly. Charles is shocked to learn that Cyrus had so much money and wonders how Cyrus could have made it honestly.

Some time later, Charles receives a telegram from Adam asking for $100 to pay for his trip home to Connecticut. Charles sends the money via a telegraph officer, who asks Charles for a specific question he can ask Adam in order to verify Adam's identity. Charles tells the telegraph officer to ask Adam what present he gave his father before enlisting in the Army. If Adam answers "a puppy," then it is definitely Adam, and the money can be transferred.

When Adam arrives at home, he is somewhat surprised to find that he no longer feels intimidated by Charles. The brothers discuss their father and their inheritance. Charles informs Adam that he has figured out that all of Cyrus's war stories were lies, for Cyrus's Army papers were sent along with his will, and the dates on them clearly indicate that Cyrus could not have fought in the noteworthy battles in which he claimed to have fought. Furthermore, Charles suspects that Cyrus's fortune may have been stolen, but Adam denies it. Adam says that he and Charles should travel to California with the money, but only after building a memorial to their father.

SUMMARY: CHAPTER 8

> *I believe there are monsters born in the world to human parents. . . . The face and body may be perfect, but if a twisted gene or a malformed egg can produce physical monsters, may not the same process produce a malformed soul?*

(See QUOTATIONS, p. 59)

Despite her innocent, childlike appearance, Cathy Ames is morally reprehensible from her earliest years. She is manipulative and selfish and learns to use her sexuality to hurt others. While still a schoolgirl, she sets up a group of local boys for punishment by luring them with her body; the boys receive a thrashing after Cathy's mother finds Cathy tied up in a barn with her skirt pulled up. Later, Cathy has a mysterious involvement with her Latin teacher that leads to his suicide.

Cathy hates her concerned parents and tries to run away to Boston. Her father catches her and beats her, which makes her more respectful and helpful around the house. One night, however, Cathy steals all the money from her father's safe, sets a fire in the house, pours chicken blood all over the floor, and locks the house from the outside on her way out. The house burns down, killing her parents, who are trapped inside. When the townspeople find the chicken blood, they believe that Cathy has been murdered.

SUMMARY: CHAPTER 9
Cathy, now using the pseudonym Catherine Amesbury, appears before Mr. Edwards, a man who runs a ring of prostitutes at inns throughout New England. The usually cold and cynical Mr. Edwards is surprised to feel a powerful sexual attraction to Cathy. Unbeknownst to his wife, he decides to keep Cathy for himself and puts her up in a small house. Cathy begins to steal from Mr. Edwards and manipulates him into fearing her.

After some time, the miserable Mr. Edwards learns something of Cathy's background. One night, he gets her drunk, and she becomes violent and threatens him with a broken wineglass. He forces her to come with him to a remote area and then beats her severely. Shocked at himself, Mr. Edwards returns home to his wife, leaving Cathy bloodied in a field that happens to be near the Trask farm in Connecticut. Cathy crawls away and eventually arrives on the Trasks' doorstep.

SUMMARY: CHAPTER 10
In the time just before Cathy's sudden arrival, Charles and Adam struggle to get along on the farm. They bicker constantly, as Adam hates Charles's insistence on waking at 4:30 every morning to work the farm (even though the inheritance from Cyrus has made them very rich), while Charles cannot stand Adam's criticism and laziness. Adam tries to talk Charles into going to California, but Charles has no interest in leaving the farm. Adam begins to leave on trips for longer and longer periods of time, traveling first to Boston and then to South America. When Adam returns from Buenos Aires, he sees that Charles has bought more land. He tells Charles the story of his months on the chain gang after the war.

SUMMARY: CHAPTER 11

Cathy crawls up to the Trasks' doorstep, covered in blood and dirt. Charles does not want to keep her in the house because he fears that it will ruin his reputation. Adam, however, says that Cathy is too weak to be sent away, so he cares for her tenderly. The sheriff questions Cathy about her beating, but she writes—she cannot speak because her jaw is broken—that she does not remember anything.

Cathy remains at the farm for some time, all the while against Charles's wishes. One day, Charles confronts her while Adam is away on an errand, telling her that he does not believe that she has really lost her memory. Charles convinces Cathy that she already told him about her past during a bout of delirium brought about by her injuries. Cathy falls for the trick, and Charles sneers at her gullibility.

Cathy believes Charles to be a great deal like her and fears him because of it. She is relieved to find that Adam, on the other hand, is easy to manipulate. When Adam suddenly asks Cathy to marry him, she considers the safe harbor that marriage would provide her and accepts his proposal, although she asks Adam not to tell Charles. Charles grows more suspicious of Cathy when a neighbor discovers a suitcase full of money and clothing near the site of her beating. But as soon as Charles leaves the house, Adam takes Cathy into town and marries her.

Charles becomes furious when he discovers that Adam and Cathy are married. Cathy is dismayed to learn that Adam intends to move her to California. That night, Cathy tells Adam that she is still too badly injured to sleep with him. She drugs Adam with a sleeping medication and then goes to Charles, who takes her into his bed.

ANALYSIS: CHAPTERS 6–11

When Cyrus Trask dies, he leaves a suspicious inheritance that threatens to taint his family for generations afterward—a symbolic parallel to the biblical idea of original sin. According to the Christian tradition, Adam and Eve are created as sinless beings and sent to live in the earthly paradise of Eden. However, they fall into sin after Satan, in the form of a serpent, tempts them into eating the fruit from the tree of knowledge of good and evil, which God has forbidden them to eat. In punishment, God curses Eve to suffer painful childbirth and to submit to her husband's authority; he curses Adam to toil and work the ground for food. Then, God banishes Adam and Eve from Eden. Adam and Eve pass this original sin on to all their descendants, who are born as already sinful beings. In

East of Eden, Cyrus's dishonestly won fortune, which he either steals or gains from a career built on lies about his supposed Civil War experience, is a symbol for this original sin. The result of Cyrus's sin—the inheritance of $100,000—literally is passed on to his sons.

After Cyrus's death, Adam and Charles live together on the farm as equals, but the vast differences in their characters and attitudes drive them apart. Charles is cynical and pragmatic, obsessed with work, money, and gain. Adam, meanwhile, is idealistic, uninterested in the financial aspects of life, and longs to travel and see the world. Furthermore, we see that Charles still resents the incident of Cyrus's birthday gifts, as he uses his memory of the event as the basis for the password that Adam must use to collect money from the telegraph official. Charles and Adam also are deeply divided in their attitudes toward their inheritance from Cyrus: Charles believes that Cyrus stole his fortune, but Adam disagrees, refusing to believe the possibility that their father could ever be dishonest. The narrator explains this disagreement as a result of the fact that Charles loved Cyrus, whereas Adam did not; he says that people are always suspicious and skeptical about those whom they love.

Steinbeck counters this argument about love, however, with his portrayal of Adam's blind, naïve devotion to the treacherous Cathy Ames. Cathy appears in this section as the novel's definitive embodiment of evil. Driven by self-hatred, desperation, and a love of pain, she destroys lives without remorse. She uses sex as a weapon, causing her lust-crazed teacher to commit suicide; in fact, later in the novel, she reveals that his depression and desperation over her rejection of him kept her up at night laughing. Cathy murders her parents and becomes a prostitute—apparently out of an insatiable need to be evil—and seems pleased with her decision, as though life as Mr. Edwards's whore is an improvement over life with her loving parents. As an embodiment of pure evil, Cathy is a perverse caricature of the biblical Eve, who first introduced sin into the world by eating the forbidden fruit. Similarly, Cathy—married, like Eve, to Adam—brings evil into Adam's world and later gives birth to Cal and Aron, two more characters who directly mirror the biblical Cain and Abel.

Charles, in contrast to Adam, is suspicious of Cathy from the start, perhaps because at some level Charles and Cathy seem to be cut from the same cloth. Thus far, Charles is the only character able to out-manipulate Cathy, and he does so to the point that she becomes frightened of him. The fact that Cathy gives herself sexually to Charles on the night of her marriage to Adam highlights her strange connection to Charles as well as the strange connection between the brothers. By the same token, the fact that Charles allows his brother's wife into his bed shows the extent of his cynicism, hypocrisy, and immorality. Charles would risk killing Cathy to get her out of his house, as keeping a woman could damage his reputation; at the same time, however, when Charles learns that Adam has been drugged and will therefore not discover Charles's treacherous adultery, he is more than willing to sleep with Cathy on his brother's wedding night. Although Charles is aware of Cathy's manipulative nature, he nonetheless gives into temptation and follows the impulse toward evil rather than good.

Part Two, Chapters 12–17

Summary: Chapter 12
The narrator discusses his view of history. He believes that the human capacity for nostalgia causes most unpleasant events to be glossed over or forgotten. He chalks up the entire nineteenth century, including the Civil War, to a great upwelling of greed and brutality. As the twentieth century began, he says, people had to forget the previous century in order to move into the next.

Summary: Chapter 13

> And this I believe: that the free, exploring mind of the individual human is the most valuable thing in the world. And this I would fight for: the freedom of the mind to take any direction it wishes, undirected.
>
> (See QUOTATIONS, p. 59)

The narrator writes that it is individuals, not groups, who accomplish great and inspired deeds. In light of this belief, he worries that the twentieth century's move toward automation and mass production will dampen the creative faculties of humankind.

Adam Trask moves Cathy, his newfound creative inspiration, to the Salinas Valley in California, despite her wishes to the contrary. The day Adam and Cathy leave, Charles drinks himself into a stupor, visits a prostitute, and weeps when he finds that the alcohol has made him impotent.

Adam meets many of the Salinas Valley locals, immediately fits in with them, and begins his search for a good plot of land to buy.

Returning home one day, he finds Cathy unconscious and nearly dead of blood loss in the bedroom. Adam fetches a doctor, who quickly realizes that Cathy is pregnant and that she has tried to abort her baby with a knitting needle. The furious doctor scolds Cathy for attempting to destroy life, but she placates him by lying that her family has a history of epilepsy and that she was afraid she would pass on her epilepsy on to her unborn child. The doctor believes Cathy and reassures her that epilepsy is not hereditary. He tells Adam that Cathy is pregnant.

Adam drives out to speak to Samuel Hamilton to get advice about a plot of land, as Adam has heard that Samuel is very knowledgeable about the valley. The two men discuss their plans for the future. The next day, Adam decides to buy an old ranch halfway between the towns of King City and San Lucas.

SUMMARY: CHAPTER 14

Olive Hamilton, one of Samuel's daughters (and the mother of the novel's narrator), becomes a teacher in order to avoid life as a ranch wife. Determined to live in a town, she refuses to marry a farmer of any kind. Finally, she marries the owner of the King City flourmill and has four children. The narrator remembers his mother as a strict, loving woman who hammered a fear of debt into her children and who nursed her son through a severe case of pneumonia.

During World War I, Olive sold Liberty bonds to support the war effort, and she did so well that the government awarded her its grandest prize—a ride in an airplane. Terrified at the thought of flying, Olive went through with the flight only for the sake of her excited children. Once in the air, the pilot misunderstood Olive's wishes and performed a number of aeronautic stunts. Dizzied and sickened after landing, Olive stayed in bed for two days.

SUMMARY: CHAPTER 15

Adam becomes deeply happy in his life in California with Cathy. He hires a Chinese-American man named Lee as a cook and housekeeper. Lee makes Cathy nervous, but she enjoys the relatively luxury of her existence nonetheless. One day, while giving Samuel a ride to the Trasks, Lee confides in Samuel that he likes being a servant because it enables him to control his master. Lee says that, although he has lived in America all his life, he uses pidgin English—sentences such as "Me talkee Chinese talk"—to play into Americans' stereotypes and expectations of him.

Adam asks Samuel to help him search for water on his land to determine if it will be good for farming. Adam tells Samuel about his past in Connecticut. Later, at dinner at the Trask house, Samuel finds himself virtually ignored by his hosts. Adam dotes on Cathy, while Cathy appears completely withdrawn into herself. After Samuel leaves, Cathy shocks Adam by telling him that she never wanted to come to California and that she plans to leave as soon as she is able. Adam tells her that things will change for her when her child is born.

SUMMARY: CHAPTER 16

Samuel likes Adam but is chilled by the inhumanity he senses in Cathy. Samuel agrees to help Adam renovate the old, decrepit house on the ranch Adam has bought. Liza, however, disapproves, for she thinks that the Trasks' wealth and idleness are marks of immorality.

SUMMARY: CHAPTER 17

One day, while Samuel is working at the Trask house, Lee appears and reports that Cathy is in labor. Lee comments that there is something unpleasant about Cathy, and Samuel agrees. Despite Cathy's overt hostility—she even bites Samuel on the hand as he attempts to help her deliver—Samuel helps her through labor, and she gives birth to twin boys. Cathy refuses to look at the infants, which prompts Samuel to tell her outright that he does not like her.

Liza goes to the Trasks' to help with the infants, and Lee also cares for the twins, despite his growing sense of foreboding about Cathy. After Cathy has rested for a week, Adam knocks on her door, and she appears at the door dressed for travel. She tells Adam that she is leaving and that she does not care what he does with the infants. Adam locks Cathy in her room. When he opens the door later, she has a gun pointed at him and shoots him in the shoulder. Adam falls to the floor and lies helplessly as the twins wail in the background.

ANALYSIS: CHAPTERS 12–17

Steinbeck opens Part Two of *East of Eden* with a meditation on the power of the individual that foreshadows some of the novel's later developments. Thus far in the novel, we have seen the characters encounter the choice between good and evil—some are clearly on the path of good, while others are on the path of evil. However, it is unclear at this point whether these characters truly have the ability to *choose* between good and evil. Charles's and Adam's personalities seem to have been determined from the time they were young boys; likewise, Steinbeck speculates that Cathy was "born" a "monster." Here, however, despite these seeming instances of predetermination, Steinbeck argues that there is nothing more valuable in the world than the "free exploring mind of the individual human." He implies a power of individual choice that is similar to the biblical idea of *timshel* that surfaces in the upcoming chapters.

The news of Cathy's pregnancy comes hand in hand with the revelation that she has attempted an abortion on her own unborn infants, which further establishes her as a demonic anti-mother figure, a perversion of the biblical Eve. In a household that should be a bed of fertility—a husband and wife living on a ranch in a particularly fertile corner of the Salinas Valley—Cathy is a cancer and a parasite. Cathy's evil constitutes more than just cunning self-interest, for it appears that some part of her actually craves debasement. Unlike the biblical Eve, who is *tricked* into committing sin, Cathy revels in sin for its own sake. Her inability to trust anyone puts her in a position of longing for control—specifically, the kind of control she can achieve through manipulation and deceit, guarding her true motivations while exploiting other people's trust.

Although the chapter about Olive Hamilton may at first seem out of place, its position directly following the chapter about Cathy's abortion attempt highlights the contrast between the Trask and Hamilton families. Whereas Cathy is evil to the core and actively tries to destroy her unborn children, Olive is a loving and nurturing figure. A teacher by profession, she has four children of her own, whom she raises sternly but with clear, loving concern for their character and well being. The story of Olive's terrifying flight in a government plane indicates the depth of her love for her family, as she undergoes the ordeal of the flight simply to please her children. Throughout *East of Eden,* Steinbeck employs such alternating chapters between the Trasks and the Hamiltons to maintain the Hamiltons as a point of contrast, even though they are not the main focus of the story.

Likewise, the personable and astute Lee provides a counterbalance to Cathy's nastiness throughout the novel. Lee provides a much-needed note of humor to the novel, as he revels that he has duped Adam and others with a thick Chinese accent even though he has grown up in America and has gone to college. More important, Lee is wise, not only on an intellectual level—he shares Samuel's love of books and philosophy—but also on an intuitive level, as we see in his justifiable distrust of Cathy. Like Charles, Lee makes Cathy nervous because he always seems to see through her schemes. The honesty and good nature that Lee exhibits infuse the otherwise barren Trask household with a sense of goodness and love, balancing the evil that emanates from Cathy. In this sense, the dynamic between Lee and Cathy is yet another microcosmic arena for the human struggle between good and evil.

PART TWO, CHAPTERS 18–22

SUMMARY: CHAPTER 18
Adam tells Horace Quinn, the local deputy sheriff, that he got his gunshot wound by accidentally shooting himself while cleaning his gun. Quinn, however, sees through Adam's story immediately. Adam begins to weep when Quinn asks about Cathy. Quinn confers with the sheriff, who says that Faye, the proprietress of a local brothel, recently asked the sheriff about a runaway who closely matches Cathy's description. Quinn and the sheriff agree to keep the news from Adam so that the twins will not know that their mother is a prostitute.

In the meantime, Samuel counsels the miserable Adam that if he acts as though he is happy and alive, eventually he will feel that way. Samuel reminds Adam that his children need his strength.

SUMMARY: CHAPTER 19
The narrator says that there are three houses of prostitution in the Salinas Valley, and that the valley residents accept these houses as an essential but undiscussed part of their society. Faye's brothel is the newest, and Cathy—now calling herself Kate—thrives there, having earned Faye's trust to quickly become an indispensable part of Faye's operation. When the sheriff finds Cathy, he tells her that as long as she agrees never to contact her sons, he will never make her background and her shooting of Adam a public matter. The sheriff also tells Cathy that he will never let his son come to Faye's, for he does not want his son ever to meet Cathy.

SUMMARY: CHAPTER 20
Faye is impressed by the fact that Cathy lectures the brothel's piano player, Cotton Eye, about his opium habit. Faye tells Cathy that Cathy has become like a daughter to her. She urges Cathy to give up prostitution, but Cathy says she needs the money.

Faye invites Cathy into her room for an elaborate ceremony in which she presents Cathy with her will. The will gives all of Faye's worldly possessions to Cathy upon Faye's death—an incredible sum, as the brothel does very well financially. Cathy is thrilled, but when she drinks a bit of Faye's celebratory champagne, she loses her inhibitions and begins to say cruel things to Faye. Cathy even confesses brazenly that she makes more money than Faye realizes, as she uses whips and razors and other sadomasochistic devices on her clients.

Faye screams in horror, and Cathy, panicking, gives her a drink to put her to sleep. Horrified by what she has revealed to Faye in her drunkenness, Cathy knocks Faye out with ammonia and pokes her with sharp instruments to make her believe that she is having a horrible nightmare. The other prostitutes believe that Cathy is caring tenderly for Faye, and when Faye wakes, she believes the same thing. Faye believes that everything Cathy told her during the night was part of her nightmare, and she is grateful for Cathy's care and sweetness.

SUMMARY: CHAPTER 21

Over time, Cathy begins to assume more and more control over Faye's house. She takes advantage of the local doctor's absentmindedness to begin slowly poisoning Faye with drugs. All the while, Cathy makes certain that the other girls believe her to be slavishly devoted to Faye. When Faye finally dies, Cathy pretends to be insensible with grief.

SUMMARY: CHAPTER 22

Adam's depression over Cathy's departure does not lift. Lee confides to Samuel that Adam still has not named his infant sons, even though they are more than a year old. Samuel finds this abominable and lectures Adam for his melancholy. The two men argue, and the typically nonviolent Samuel strikes Adam with his fist in an attempt to jolt him out of his stupor. The tactic appears to work, and Samuel tells Adam that they must sit down and name the two infant boys.

The men look over the baby boys and discuss possible names for them. Samuel brings up the biblical story of Cain and Abel. Then, looking in a Bible, he suggests Joshua and Caleb as names for the boys. One of the boys cries when he hears the word Caleb, which Adam takes as a sign. The first boy, therefore, is named Caleb. Adam dislikes the name Joshua because Joshua was a warrior, so he chooses the name Aaron for his second boy. This choice pleases

Samuel, even though he knows that the biblical Aaron never made it to the Promised Land (Canaan, or modern Israel). The second child cries out when he hears the name Aaron, which Adam takes as another sign, so the second boy is named Aaron.

ANALYSIS: CHAPTERS 18–22

The discussion of Cain and Abel during the naming of the twins explicitly invokes the biblical story that underlies all of *East of Eden* and its exploration of the struggle between good and evil. While naming the boys, Samuel, Lee, and Adam discuss the conflict between good and evil that exists throughout human civilization and within every individual. Adam remarks that the first time he read the story of Cain and Abel, he remembers feeling "a little outraged at God" because of the arbitrariness of God's decision to favor Abel over Cain. Adam fails to see, however, the similarity between the story and his own life, especially Cyrus's seemingly arbitrary favoring of Adam over Charles. Adam's failure to make the connection is striking, as he clearly is aware that the Cain and Abel story has played itself out repeatedly in the countless generations of human history. Later, we see that Adam's unawareness continues, as he himself favors one of his boys over the other in the same manner as his father.

In the whorehouse, not far away, Cathy takes her scheming to an unprecedented level as she engineers Faye's demise. We learn that Cathy practices sadomasochism on her clients, using knives and whips to debase the human body further and to give vent to the uncontrollable evil inside her. We see once again, as we see earlier in her interactions with Mr. Edwards, that alcohol strips Cathy of her control, inducing her to confess her true feelings as she reveals her schemes to Faye. Perhaps the most appalling part of this section is the lengths to which Cathy goes to convince Faye—after drugging Faye, abusing her sleeping body, poisoning her with ammonia, and poking her with sharp objects in her sleep—that it was all just a nightmare. When the business finally becomes hers, Cathy runs it with an iron fist, keeping the prostitutes in constant fear of her rather than cultivating the somewhat motherly dynamic that Faye had established.

Cathy's evil is so thorough and unrelenting that at times it may come across as implausible, especially since it does not appear that Cathy uses her evil acts to attain any sort of ultimate goal or aim. Indeed, many literary critics have taken Steinbeck to task in his portrayal of Cathy, claiming that the seeming totality of her evil undermines her believability as a character. When a family friend wrote to Steinbeck that he did not believe Cathy "because she was all bad," Steinbeck replied, "I don't know whether I believe her either but I know she exists." Early in the novel, Steinbeck writes that Cathy is "indecipherable," and to a large degree he does not attempt to explain her aside from his theory he advances that she was "born" evil. Most critics to this day, however, have not accepted Steinbeck's vagueness in the matter, and the bulk of critics of *East of Eden* focus on Cathy as the novel's major flaw.

PART THREE, CHAPTERS 23–26

SUMMARY: CHAPTER 23

In 1911, Samuel is stricken with grief after his favorite daughter, Una, dies shortly after moving to a remote area of Oregon with her husband. When the Hamilton children visit Samuel and Liza for Thanksgiving, they notice that the previously youthful Samuel has suddenly aged significantly. The children devise a plan get their parents off the ranch by taking turns hosting them for long periods of time. Tom disapproves of the plan, saying it indicates to the aged Samuel that his life is essentially over. The other children, however, like the plan and present the idea to Samuel as though it were a vacation. Samuel accepts the plan but confides to Tom that he sees through it and realizes that his children are helping him transition into old age.

SUMMARY: CHAPTER 24

> "[T]he Hebrew word, the word timshel— 'Thou mayest'—that gives a choice. It might be the most important word in the world. That says the way is open"
>
> *(See* QUOATIONS, *p. 60)*

Before he leaves his farm to stay with his children, Samuel goes to see Adam Trask. Samuel talks to the twins, now eleven years old, and reflects upon the fact that the easygoing Aron (he has dropped the first A in Aaron) reminds him of Abel and the closemouthed Caleb reminds him of Cain.

Samuel, Adam, and Lee discuss the biblical story of Cain and Abel. Lee says that he has been troubled by a discrepancy in the story that arises from two different translations of the Bible—according to one translation, God *promises* Cain that he will overcome sin; in another translation, God *orders* Cain to overcome sin. According to Lee, the Hebrew word in question is *timshel.* After researching the matter for several years, Lee has determined that *timshel* means "thou mayest." Lee considers this translation of *timshel* to be an extraordinary revelation, as it implies that God has given human beings the *choice* of whether or not to overcome sin—essentially giving humans the freedom to choose their course in life.

The men go for a walk, and Samuel asks Adam if he is happy. Adam does not answer. Samuel, hoping to force Adam to forget about Cathy, reveals to Adam that Cathy runs the most depraved whorehouse in the entire valley. Overcome with shock, Adam hurries away.

SUMMARY: CHAPTER 25
Samuel Hamilton dies of old age. After the funeral, Adam goes to Cathy's brothel. As soon as he sees that Cathy is no longer beautiful and that she is actually a monster, Adam realizes that he finally can put her out of his mind. When he tells her as much, she responds that he is wrong to condemn her for her views, for there is nothing but depravity and evil in the world.

Cathy shows Adam photos of some of the most powerful and important men of the Salinas Valley performing sadomasochistic sex acts with her whores, and she brazenly admits to blackmailing the men with the pictures. As Adam rises to leave, Cathy suddenly panics, feeling him slip away—she even offers to sleep with him. When Adam shudders in disgust, Cathy cruelly claims that Charles is the twins' real father, for she slept with Charles on the night of her marriage to Adam. Adam says that he does not believe her and that it does not matter anyway, even if she is telling the truth.

Cathy screams, and the brothel's bouncer comes in and knocks Adam down. Even so, Adam leaves with a serene smile on his face, realizing that he is finally free of the burden of Cathy that has been on his mind for so many years.

SUMMARY: CHAPTER 26
Adam rides the train back from Salinas. Happy about his encounter with Cathy, he stops in at Will Hamilton's car dealership and tells Will he would like to buy a car. At home, Adam tells Lee that he now plans to make something of his land and to strengthen his relationship with his sons. Lee confesses that he hopes to leave the valley

soon to start a bookstore in San Francisco but agrees to stay in Salinas to help Adam for the time being.

ANALYSIS: CHAPTERS 23–26

One of the most important moments in the novel occurs during Samuel's second visit to Adam's home, when the men discuss the Cain and Abel story again, and Lee introduces the concept of *timshel*. *Timshel* is the Hebrew word—meaning "thou mayest"—that God speaks to Cain about overcoming sin; it suggests that it is Cain's choice whether to embrace goodness or evil. Lee considers *timshel* to be a powerful idea about human free will, something that gives people the freedom to forge their own moral destinies. The question of the validity of this idea of *timshel*, or freedom to choose between good and evil, recurs throughout the novel. Ultimately, Steinbeck offers hope that no one is predestined to evil, despite the evil and sin in the world. No individual is simply doomed to inherit the sins of his or her parents—as a number of characters, most notably Cal fear—but instead have the power to choose their own actions.

Samuel's final gift to Adam is the revelation of the truth about Cathy. When Adam visits Cathy at the brothel after Samuel's death, their conversation takes the form of a direct confrontation between good and evil. Cathy insists that there is only evil in the world; as evidence, she shows Adam pictures of seemingly righteous senators and ministers she has photographed committing demeaning sexual acts. Adam, however, now sees through Cathy, and her perverse attitude no longer threatens him. The idea of *timshel* liberates him, and after seeing her depravity, he suddenly feels that he no longer needs her. As Cathy feels her control of Adam slipping away, she becomes increasingly desperate, as though her loss of control over Adam measures the failure of her decision to live for sin and evil. Cathy resorts to an attempt to use sex to control Adam, but he no longer finds her beautiful, and the idea of sleeping with her actually disgusts him. Even Cathy's claim that Charles is the twins' real father—a possibility that the novel leaves open—does not faze Adam or hurt him. Ultimately, Cathy is wholly powerless over Adam, who leaves with a peaceful smile on his face. This scene represents an important turning point in the novel, as it marks the first time that good (represented by Adam) confronts evil (represented by Cathy) without fear. Notably, this episode is also the first time that good emerges in triumph. Evil needs good—as evidenced by

Charles's desperate need to have Adam around, and here in Cathy's need to control Adam—but the converse does not hold true: when liberated by the idea of *timshel,* good does not need evil.

PART THREE, CHAPTERS 27–33

SUMMARY: CHAPTER 27

Aron and Cal (the nickname he has taken for Caleb) play outside, hunting rabbits. The narrator discusses the differences between them: Aron is good-natured and handsome, while Cal is manipulative and vague. The boys discuss their mother. Cal says that he has heard rumors that their mother is in Salinas, not in heaven, as Adam has told them. Enraged, Aron attacks Cal, who realizes that he has found something that gives him power over Aron—Aron's feelings for their mother.

At home, the boys discover that they have visitors, the Bacons, who were passing by and have been caught in a sudden downpour. Mr. Bacon suggests to Adam that he rent out his farm and move to town if he does not intend to farm the land. Adam, lost in his own stream of thought, ponders taking the boys to visit his brother, Charles, whom they have never met.

Outside, the boys play with the Bacons' daughter, Abra, who is kind to Aron, much to Cal's annoyance. Cal offers to give Abra the rabbit he shot that day; Aron replies that it is his rabbit, but that Abra may take it home to bury it if she likes. Abra agrees. When Aron leaves, Cal makes up lies to upset Abra. Cal says that Lee beats Aron and that Aron is going to put a snake in the box rather than the dead rabbit.

As the Bacons drive away, Abra throws the box out of their buggy, which hurts Aron's feelings—he has put a love note inside the box for her. Cal offers to give Aron his rifle if he wants to shoot Abra, but Aron points out that Cal does not have a rifle.

SUMMARY: CHAPTER 28

That night at dinner, the normally distant Adam surprises the boys by suddenly asking them questions, showing interest in them, and treating them with kindness. Cal asks where their mother is buried, and Adam lies that she was sent back to her home in the east.

Later, Lee tells Adam not to lie to the boys, for they will discover the truth one day, and in lying, Adam risks injuring their trust. Lee then talks about his own childhood. His mother and father worked on the railroads, his pregnant mother having disguised herself as a man so she could join her husband on the voyage to the United States. After she gave birth to Lee, a mob of the other (all male) railroad workers, shocked that she was a woman, raped and killed her. But then, feeling instant remorse and revulsion at their deed, the railroad workers raised Lee as one of their own.

Adam writes a loving letter to Charles asking him to visit California. He worries about how Charles will interpret the letter and impatiently waits for a reply.

SUMMARY: CHAPTER 29
Will Hamilton arrives at the Trask house with Adam's new car, but neither Will nor the mechanic who comes the next day seems to understand how the car works.

SUMMARY: CHAPTER 30
Adam finally figures out the car and drives the boys into town in order to check his mail. In the mail is a letter from attorneys in Connecticut announcing that Charles has died and left a fortune of $100,000 to be split between Adam and Cathy.

Adam consults Lee about the inheritance, unable to understand why Charles would leave money to someone he despised. Cal eavesdrops on Adam and Lee's conversation. Lee observes that Cathy is not likely to claim the money, but he notes that his advice is probably irrelevant because he is sure that Adam will give Cathy the money anyway.

Lee announces that he is feeling old and that he wants to go to San Francisco to open a bookstore. The overheard conversation makes Cal sad, and he prays to God to become more like Aron. Trying to be kind, Cal tells Aron that Adam plans to send a wreath to their mother's grave. Cal gets into bed and continues to pray to God to make him better.

SUMMARY: CHAPTER 31
Adam goes to see Cathy at the brothel to inform her about Charles's death and about her share of the fortune. Cathy is skeptical about Adam's motives for telling her about the money, for she knows full well that he could have kept it for himself and never told her. Adam confronts Cathy, telling her that she is only "part of a human" and that she simply is incapable of believing that there is any good in the world. This touches a nerve with Cathy, who shakes in rage as Adam leaves.

On an impulse, Adam then goes to visit Liza Hamilton, who is currently staying in Salinas with her daughter Olive, who is married to a man named Ernest Steinbeck (the narrator's father). Adam tells Liza that he is thinking of moving the twins into town.

SUMMARY: CHAPTER 32

After his father's death, Tom Hamilton lives in the old ranch house and secretly writes melancholy poetry. After a time, his sister Dessie decides to come live with him, and he happily tells her that they will rejuvenate the old house. Tom paints the house and cleans everything thoroughly, but Dessie begins to suffer from intense stomach pains, the severity of which she attempts to hide from Tom.

SUMMARY: CHAPTER 33

Tom and Dessie decide to raise money for a trip abroad, and Tom hits upon the idea of making money by raising young pigs. When he returns from a trip into town to see Will about borrowing money for the pig business, however, he finds Dessie doubled over with pain. Tom gives her salts to drink—a traditional remedy—and calls a doctor. The doctor curses Tom, telling him that giving her salts was a mistake that likely has made Dessie's ailment even worse. As the doctor steps out his door, he tells his wife to call Will Hamilton and inform him that he must drive the doctor to Tom's house, as his sister is dying.

Dessie dies. Tom, sick with grief and guilt that he may have inadvertently caused her death, deliriously tells his father's spirit that he wants to commit suicide. Tom writes a letter to his mother, telling her that he has decided to try to break in a wild new horse that he bought. He then writes a letter to Will instructing him to say, for their mother's sake, that Tom was killed by a fall from a horse. After posting the letters, Tom shoots himself with his revolver and dies.

ANALYSIS: CHAPTERS 27–33

The Trask family strengthens as Cathy's hold over Adam weakens. Now that Adam is free from Cathy's spell, he emerges with a burst of enthusiasm and vitality, buying a car, writing to Charles, and committing himself to becoming a better father in an attempt to avoid the mistakes of his own father, Cyrus. Adam's determination not to repeat his father's mistakes is evidence that Adam believes in the idea of *timshel*. At first, the twins can hardly believe that their reserved, melancholy father is suddenly interested and excited about their lives. However, once they realize that a permanent change seems to have come over Adam, they respond by talking with him and loving him more.

Aron and Cal, respectively, bear striking similarities to the young Adam and Charles we see early in the novel. Aron has a light complexion and is kind, trusting, and open; Cal has a dark complexion and is manipulative, suspicious, and conflicted. Cal is deeply jealous of Aron and intentionally tries to hurt anyone who seems to love Aron more than him, as we see in Cal's tormenting of Abra. Additionally, we see that the twins are old enough to wonder about their mother, and Steinbeck slowly builds suspense as Cal accumulates evidence that Cathy is still alive. Much of the dramatic tension in this portion of the novel stems from the sense of foreboding Steinbeck creates and our trepidation that either or both of the twins will one day meet their mother.

The relationship between Cal and Aron is the most powerful and complete retelling of the Cain and Abel story in *East of Eden*—with the key difference that Cal, the Cain character, seems open to the idea of *timshel* and thus may be able to overcome his mother's legacy and live morally. So far, every major character in *East of Eden* has fit into the dichotomy of good and evil, with Adam, Samuel, and Lee falling in the former, and Cathy, Charles, and Cyrus in the latter. Aron appears destined to be good like his father, whereas Cal appears destined for evil like his mother and uncle. Cal's prayers to God to make him kinder and better, however, differentiate him from his predecessors, as he recognizes his evil ways and fights to control them.

Although most of the main ideas and themes of *East of Eden* play themselves out within the Trask family, the Hamiltons continue to be of crucial importance to the novel. Steinbeck uses the Hamiltons not only to portray the world in which he himself was brought up and to contrast with the Trasks, but also to portray his idea of historical evolution. In one key passage, Steinbeck reflects on the origin of prostitution by remarking that a new frontier is always settled first by brave, wild, innocent men, who are soon followed by bankers, lawyers, and businessmen. The first generation of Hamiltons, represented by Samuel and Liza, is clearly in the category of brave innocents. The second generation of Hamiltons appears split between the passion and goodness handed down by Samuel and Liza and the commercial spirit of the bankers, lawyers, and businessmen, which Will clearly embodies. In this section, Dessie and Tom—the Hamiltons who most embody the spirit of their parents—

come to tragic ends, leaving the overly business-minded and conservative Will as the main representative of the Hamiltons in the later parts of the novel.

The circumstances of Dessie's death and Tom's suicide add a faint, ironic echo to the story of Cain and Abel as it recurs throughout *East of Eden*. Tom plays a part in killing his sibling by giving her salts when he should not have done so. But unlike Cain, who tries to deny responsibility for Abel's death, Tom takes too much responsibility, blaming himself for Dessie's death when he really only committed an innocent and well-meaning mistake. Tom represents a sort of anti-Cain, whose essential goodness leads him to blame himself for being evil when he is not evil. This reversal also echoes the story of Cyrus Trask's first wife—Adam's mother—who committed suicide after contracting syphilis and left a suicide note confessing to sins that she had not committed. However, in the moral judgment of the novel, Tom's suicide clearly represents a tragic error; as Lee tells Cal later, it is important for guilty people to realize that they are simply normal, flawed human beings, not abstract abominations of evil. Although the idea of *timshel* might have enabled Tom to grieve for Dessie but then go on with his life, Tom does not accept or recognize this idea and instead takes his penance to a tragic extreme.

PART FOUR, CHAPTERS 34–40

SUMMARY: CHAPTER 34

> *I believe that there is one story in the world. . . . Humans are caught . . . in a net of good and evil. . . . There is no other story.*
>
> (See QUOTATIONS, *p. 60*)

The narrator discusses the struggle between good and evil, which he says is the one recurring narrative of human history. He says that people can be measured by the world's reaction to their deaths. He remembers one man who made a fortune on the backs of others but then attempted to make it up later by becoming a philanthropist; people took that man's death with quiet relief. He remembers a second man who had always been immoral, manipulating others under the pretense of virtue; people greeted his death with joy. Finally, the narrator remembers a third man who made many errors but who devoted his life to giving others strength in a time of great need; when he died, people burst into incredible grief.

SUMMARY: CHAPTER 35

The Trasks move to Salinas proper, buying the house in which Dessie Hamilton lived before she moved to the ranch with Tom. Lee leaves to open his bookstore in San Francisco. Aron and Cal discuss Lee's departure, and Aron bets Cal ten cents that Lee will come back. Aron wins the bet, as Lee returns only six days later. Lee tells Adam that he was lonesome, that he realized he really did not want to run a bookstore, and that he is very glad to be home.

SUMMARY: CHAPTER 36

Aron and Cal begin school in Salinas and are assigned to the seventh grade. They quickly prove themselves to be bright, popular students. Aron is well liked, whereas Cal bullies his way into respect on the playground.

After the first day of school, Aron follows Abra Bacon to her house and asks her to marry him someday. She takes him to a secret place—a canopy of leaves beneath a willow tree—where she says they can practice being married. Abra asks Aron about his mother and pretends to be his mother herself by laying his head in her lap. He begins to cry. Abra tells Aron that she overheard her parents saying that Aron's mother is still alive. Aron does not believe her because it would mean that Adam and Lee have lied to him. Abra gives Aron a kiss before she leaves.

SUMMARY: CHAPTER 37

In 1915, Lee buys an icebox for the family, which starts Adam thinking about a possible way to make money: packing produce in ice and shipping it in refrigerated train cars to areas of the country that normally cannot get perishable produce during the winter. Will Hamilton tells Adam that his idea is foolish, but Adam tries it anyway. The scheme is a disaster, as the train is delayed at every turn, and the Salinas lettuce that Adam ships arrives rotten and late in the east, just as the skeptics predicted.

After the shipping boondoggle, Adam's once-sizable fortune is depleted to the point that he only has $9,000 to his name. Aron and Cal become the butt of jokes at school, and Adam is the laughing stock of the town. Only Abra stands by Aron, promising never to desert him. Cal, increasingly jealous of the time Abra and Aron spend together, becomes frustrated and restless. Because Adam is no longer universally respected in town, rumors begin to spread about Cathy and about Adam's past. Abra overhears one such rumor and advises Aron to ask his father about his mother, but Aron nervously declines.

SUMMARY: CHAPTER 38

Cal becomes increasingly restless and starts to wander outdoors at night. On one such excursion, a drunken farmer named Rabbit Holman tells Cal about his mother's brothel and even takes Cal there. Appalled, Cal returns home and tells Lee what he has seen, and Lee tells Cal the full truth about Cathy. Lee says that Cal's mother is almost inhumanly evil. Cal worries that he has inherited this evil, but Lee urges Cal to remember that he has free will in all his behavior—that he, not his mother, will determine his path in life.

Cal tries to dedicate himself to a moral life, but temptation consistently causes him to stray. He does not tell Aron about their mother, as he fears that the news would destroy the good and trusting Aron. Aron, in the meantime, has discovered religion and says he has decided to become a minister. He even tells Abra that he wishes to remain celibate. Abra humors him, for she assumes that he will change his mind by the time she is ready to marry him.

SUMMARY: CHAPTER 39

A wave of moral reform sweeps Salinas—as the narrator notes, this occurs every few years—and organized gambling comes under fire within the town. Cal likes to watch the gambling during his nocturnal wanderings, and one night he is arrested during a police raid. When Adam retrieves Cal from the prison, the father and son have a long, heartfelt talk. Adam confesses that he thinks he is a bad father to the boys, and Cal confesses that he knows the truth about Cathy. Adam and Cal discuss Aron. Cal thinks that Aron's deep, innate goodness makes him fragile and that therefore he needs to be protected. Cal promises never to tell Aron about their mother.

Cal feels much closer to his father after their talk. He begins to spy on the brothel to learn about Cathy and gradually notices that she follows exactly the same schedule every Monday. Cal begins to follow Cathy around. She gives no sign that she notices him until she suddenly confronts him one Monday and asks why he has been following her. Cal tells Cathy that he is her son, and she takes him inside the brothel to talk.

In her room, Cathy keeps the light off, for she says that it hurts her eyes. She also wears bandages on her hands because of her severe arthritis. Cathy asks Cal about his brother and his father. Cal refuses to talk about Adam but says that Aron is doing well. Enraged to see how much Cal loves his brother and his father, Cathy brags to Cal about her ability to manipulate and control people. She insinuates that she and Cal are very much alike. Cal asks his mother whether, when she was a child, she ever felt that everyone else understood something that she did not. A strange look passes over Cathy's face, and Cal suddenly realizes that he does not have to be like his mother. He tells her that he knows the light does not hurt her eyes—rather, the light makes her afraid.

SUMMARY: CHAPTER 40

One day, Cathy receives a visit from a woman named Ethel, who was a prostitute at the brothel when Faye was still in charge. Ethel implies that she found the discarded bottles of poison that Cathy used to kill Faye and tries to blackmail Cathy for $100 a month to keep the secret. Cathy, however, uses her influence to have Ethel arrested and sent out of the county for theft. Nevertheless, Cathy begins to feel increasingly nervous that Ethel will turn her in. She also begins to sense the presence of Charles Trask around her. She feels increasingly paranoid and restless.

ANALYSIS: CHAPTERS 34–40

Here, Steinbeck returns his focus to the Trask family, specifically to Aron and Cal, who have become the main characters of the second half of the novel. The perception that Cal is the bad child and Aron is the good child—that they are the Cain and Abel of their generation—still exists, but Cal continually undermines this assumption as we see him struggle to be good. Cal's conversation with his father after his arrest underscores the boy's capacity for love, which is in some ways to blame for his belief in his own evil. Indeed, Cal loves those around him so much that he believes he cannot be worthy of them; when he sees that other people like Aron better than him, it makes him hate Aron and hate himself—seeming to confirm Cal's fear that he is unworthy. However, Cal's conversation with Adam is a step in the right direction, and it brings father and son closer together.

Cal shows his newfound strength and moral compass when he stands up to Cathy in their climactic first meeting. Despite his mother's questioning, Cal refuses to talk to her about Adam. Moreover, Cal displays considerable intuition in recognizing the fear that lies behind Cathy's façade of bragging and flattery. In part, Cal's strength stems from the fact that he understands what it is like to be both good and evil: he is tormented by the same demons that haunt Cathy but is able to overcome them as Cathy cannot. As a result, Cal is able to withstand the knowledge that his mother is a prostitute—a revelation that would likely crush the sensitive Aron, who would have no means of understanding or enduring his mother. Later in the novel, Abra is the first character to recognize this struggling aspect of Cal's personality, and she tells Cal that she loves him because of it.

Aron forfeits some of his standing in our eyes in this section, as his decision to join the church and his declaration to Abra that he intends to remain celibate strike jarring notes. We sense that Aron, rather than face the realities of the world, wants only to build a barrier around himself to hide from these realities. Both Cal and Adam perceive that Aron's goodness makes him fragile, as he is unable to endure the knowledge of the evil in the world. Aron's newfound religious fervor comes across as false and affected, a thinly disguised attempt to steep himself in an unthreatening fantasy world. Steinbeck portrays Abra, meanwhile, as a likable and appealing girl, full of love and common sense. In this light, Aron's rejection of her appears both cowardly and foolish. At the same time, Aron also distances himself from his father: Adam's failed business venture shames Aron, who is embarrassed to be associated with it. Cal, on the other hand, rallies to support his father and even becomes determined to earn back all the money Adam has lost. Although Aron is still largely the Abel figure and Cal the Cain figure, Steinbeck does a great deal in these chapters to confound our expectations of those associations. As *East of Eden* progresses, he pins the moral hopes of the novel squarely on Cain.

Part Four, Chapters 41–44

Summary: Chapter 41

As it appears that war may break out in Europe, Cal convinces Aron to finish high school and begin college early. Cal even promises to help Aron pay for college. When Lee finds out about Cal's plan, he offers to help with $5,000 he has saved over the years. Then, Cal talks to Will Hamilton about making money. Will is impressed with Cal's openness and pragmatic business sense. Will takes Cal out to the Trask ranch and asks whether he wants a business partner. He tells Cal about a plan he has to make a great deal of money exporting beans in the wartime economy.

After the war breaks out, patriotic spirit explodes in Salinas. Cal and Will buy beans from local farmers for two-and-a-half cents a pound and sell them in England for twelve cents a pound. Cal plans to make enough money to restore the fortune Adam lost in his botched attempt at the refrigerated shipping business.

SUMMARY: CHAPTER 42

The narrator briefly discusses the onset of World War I and how it affects Salinas. Telegrams begin to arrive informing families that their sons have been killed—a reality that gradually destroys the townspeople's myth that the war could never affect them directly.

SUMMARY: CHAPTER 43

Adam, proud of Aron's decision to finish high school early, tells Lee that he wishes Cal had the same ambition. Lee replies that Cal may surprise Adam. Aron, busy with his studies in school and at church, hears that a local madam has begun attending church services.

The war continues, and Liza Hamilton dies. Aron passes his graduation exams but does not tell his father; Aron tells Cal that he does not think his father would even care about the exams. Lee, however, tells Aron that his father is immensely proud and that he was planning to give Aron a gold watch for graduation.

SUMMARY: CHAPTER 44

Abra starts to spend time with Lee and Adam after Aron leaves for Stanford University. She confides in Lee and asks him if it is true that Aron's mother is a prostitute. Lee confesses that it is indeed true. He worries that Aron will find out and that he will never understand that Adam lied to him about it in order to protect him. Meanwhile, Cal tells Lee that he has made enough money to pay back his $5,000, along with an additional $15,000 on top of it. Cal plans to give the money to his father on Thanksgiving.

One day, Abra tells Cal that Aron said he does not want to marry her, for he wants to be in the clergy. Cal says that Aron might still change his mind. Abra asks Cal if he visits prostitutes, and Cal confesses that he does. Abra tells Cal that she is sinful too, but Cal is skeptical. He tells Abra that life with Aron will force her to be moral.

ANALYSIS: CHAPTERS 41–44

These transitional chapters continue to undermine our original assumption that Aron is destined for good and Cal for evil. Instead, both boys exercise the free will implied by the concept of *timshel,* although they do so to different ends: Aron chooses a life of security and illusion, while Cal struggles to be moral amid the realities and evils of the world.

Cal encounters several important moral decision points in these chapters, and we see that he does not always choose well, despite his good motivations. Cal's desperation to make back his father's lost fortune leads him to go along with Will Hamilton's morally dubious scheme to make money on the bean market in the wartime economy. The scheme, though legal, amounts to war profiteering, as it involves buying beans at cheap prices from California farmers who have no buyers and reselling the beans at high prices to English consumers whose wartime rations are running short. In addition to his questionable business dealings, Cal also admits that he frequents prostitutes. However, Cal's decision to go along with Will's scheme is grounded in love for Adam, and his decision to visit prostitutes illustrates that Cal, unlike Aron, lives in the real world and does the best he can with temptation. The celibate, indulgently idealistic Aron simply cuts himself off from temptation by withdrawing from the world, which comes across as a somewhat of an escape.

Adam, meanwhile, continues to place all his stock in Aron, despite the fact that Cal is the one who has the courage to struggle with and face the problems of the real world. Just as his own father, Cyrus, arbitrarily favored Adam over Charles, Adam himself now idealizes Aron and fails to see the promise in Cal. Adam mistakes Aron's flight to Stanford as ambition, failing to realize that it is just another form of escape. He lavishes expensive graduation presents on Aron while lamenting the fact that Cal does not share Aron's seeming drive and ambition. Lee, however, sees the potential in Cal and tells Adam, rightly, that Cal may surprise him one day.

PART FOUR, CHAPTERS 45–50

SUMMARY: CHAPTER 45

The narrator introduces us to a man named Joe Valery, an ex-convict who escaped from San Quentin and who now works as a pimp and bouncer for Cathy. He has looked for weaknesses in her but can find none. As a result, Joe has developed an admiration for Cathy that stems from fear.

The arthritis pain in Cathy's hands has become so severe that she begins to rely heavily on Joe to run the brothel. Because she knows the secret about his convict past, she believes that she be able to control him. Nonetheless, he continues to constantly search for a way to manipulate and outwit her. Cathy sends Joe to find Ethel in the hopes that he will bring the prostitute back to Salinas and kill her before she can tell anyone about the bottles of poison Cathy used to murder Faye. Joe asks around about Ethel in the surrounding towns and counties and discovers that she is dead already. He tells Cathy, however, that he heard a rumor that Ethel is returning to Salinas in secret. The news terrifies Cathy.

SUMMARY: CHAPTER 46
The people of Salinas are in a patriotic fever over the war. One day, a crowd, including the narrator and his sister, torments the local tailor because he has a German accent; they even set fire to the man's shop.

SUMMARY: CHAPTER 47
Adam is appointed to the local draft board, but he experiences intense guilt for sending young men away, possibly to their deaths. Lee reminds Adam of the concept of *timshel*: it is Adam's choice, Lee implies, whether or not to work for the draft board. Adam is excited for Aron to come home from Stanford for Thanksgiving; he has decided that Aron is smarter and better than Cal, unaware of the fact that Aron is miserable at Stanford.

SUMMARY: CHAPTER 48
Joe Valery continues to scheme to manipulate Cathy with the specter of Ethel and her blackmail. Cathy, meanwhile, schemes to uncover Joe's attempt to betray her. The pain in Cathy's hands has become so severe that she wears a vial of morphine capsules around her neck in case she ever wants to commit suicide.

SUMMARY: CHAPTER 49
When Aron arrives in Salinas, he is depressed and unhappy about his father's doting expectations for him. Cal, meanwhile, wraps up the $15,000 he plans to give to his father. He is nervous about Adam's response to the gift and wants desperately for his father to like it. When Adam opens the gift at Thanksgiving and sees the money, he is shocked and asks Cal how he earned it. When Adam learns about the bean-reselling operation, he becomes angry and tells Cal to return the money to the farmers he robbed in his war profiteering.

Cal turns away and runs to his room, full of anger and jealousy for Aron. Lee tells Cal to control his reaction, and Cal does finally recognize that it is within his power to control himself. He apologizes to his father and goes to see Aron, who is on his way back from Abra's house. Still roiling with jealousy, Cal tells Aron that he has something to show him. He takes Aron to see Cathy at her brothel. The next morning, Aron signs up for the army, too sickened by the truth to want to live.

SUMMARY: CHAPTER 50

The next day, Cathy is practically catatonic with the memory of Aron's visit and his horror upon learning the truth about her. She sends a note to the sheriff advising him to check Joe Valery's fingerprints and then writes a will in which she leaves all her worldly possessions to Aron. Cathy remembers her childhood, when she used to fantasize about forming a friendship with Alice of *Alice in Wonderland*. Cathy takes the morphine pill and imagines herself shrinking like Alice until she dies.

Joe Valery discovers Cathy's body the next morning and finds the will she has written. He takes the keys to Cathy's safe deposit box at the bank, as well as the photographs of the men she blackmails. However, just as Joe is about to leave the house, the sheriff's deputy arrives and says that he has to bring Joe in to see the sheriff about something—the sheriff has read Cathy's letter. Joe suddenly breaks away and tries to run, but the deputy guns him down as he flees.

ANALYSIS: CHAPTERS 46–50

On a biblical level, Adam's rejection of Cal's money parallels God's rejection of Cain's offering of grain—the act that prompts Cain to kill Abel out of jealousy. Furthermore, Adam's rejection of Cal's gift parallels Cyrus's rejection of Charles's gift earlier in the novel. In both cases, a father ignores the intentions of a loving son in order to focus on the son he has chosen to love better. In the early parts of the novel, Adam shows no love for Cyrus, while Charles loves Cyrus deeply; nonetheless, Cyrus idealizes Adam as the perfect son and prefers him to Charles. Similarly, Cal loves Adam more completely and selflessly than the anemic Aron, but Adam is so pleased with Aron's matriculation at Stanford that he decides Aron can do no wrong. His strict sense of morality prevents Adam from accepting the money from Cal; he does not take the time to realize that Cal means well by giving him the money and that Cal merely has not thought about the moral complications of the way he earned it. Similarly, when Aron learns the truth about Cathy, his despair stems largely from the fact that his father lied to him so many years by claiming his mother was dead. Aron, who lives in a world of moral simplicity and extremity, is unable to understand that Adam lied to him in order to protect him and to shield his feelings.

When Cal takes Aron to Cathy's brothel, he at least temporary loses his struggle with evil. In doing so, Cal fulfills his role in the Cain-Abel story, causing Aron to join the army and ship off to die in the war. Indeed, Cal brings Aron to their mother out of anger and a desire to inflict pain on his brother, not out of a desire to help Aron confront the ghosts of their family's past. As expected, the revelation about Cathy shatters Aron: Cathy describes Aron's horrible screaming when he sees her and Cal's bitter laughter at the sight. However, although Cal has chosen evil once again, it is significant that *East of Eden* does not end with Aron's disappearance: there is still time left for Cal to come to grips with his sin and make a decision about how he will direct his life. Cal must decide whether to choose goodness and strength or to give into the example of Cathy, whose spirit he feels inside him.

Cathy's downfall, meanwhile, is precipitous. She becomes increasingly paranoid and suspicious until the point where she actually feels Charles Trask's spirit inside her. Mirroring the emotional and psychological decay wrought by her life's commitment to evil, her body degenerates as well. Her hands are ravaged by arthritis, she suffers from insomnia, and she fears exposure to light. The extraordinary pain she has inflicted on others simply for the sake of doing so now begins to come back to haunt her. As Cathy deteriorates, she relies upon increasingly desperate means to control those around her. As she realizes that she has no control over Cal, just as she has no control over Adam, she escapes in the only manner available—a morphine overdose. A vestige of her remains, however, in the form of the inheritance that she passes to Aron.

The fortune that Cathy leaves to Aron, the third such inheritance in the novel, is a symbol of the sin that has run through the Trask family ever since Cyrus's original dishonesty and embezzlement. Cyrus leaves his tainted inheritance to Charles and Adam, and then Charles leaves an inheritance to Adam and Cathy. As a result, Cyrus's fortune forms the core of Charles's, and Charles's then forms the core of Cathy's. This family money represents an extraordinary legacy of dishonesty and evil passed down through the generations—Cyrus's was likely earned through theft, and Cathy's was earned through theft, extortion, and prostitution. The inheritance thus becomes a symbol of the idea that the sin of one generation is passed onto the next—the idea of original sin that came about when Adam and Eve were expelled from Eden. In this light, Adam, in a way, proves his essential goodness by squandering his own fortune; Cyrus, Charles, and Cathy, on the other hand, come across as evil by virtue of the fact that they increase their own fortunes. This idea of inherited sin is what makes Aron unable to stand the sight of his mother as a prostitute. Aron believes, as Cal has throughout the novel, that Cathy's wickedness taints him morally and inevitably dooms him to evil.

In every prior instance of an inheritance in *East of Eden*, the money is divided evenly between two people, diffusing the legacy of sin that the money represents. In the case of Cathy's fortune, however, Aron is the sole inheritor. Because Aron so fully accepts the idea of hereditary sin when the sight of Cathy crushes him, it is appropriate that the symbolic legacy of sin—the inheritance—should fall squarely upon his shoulders and his alone. Cal, on the other hand, receives no part of his mother's legacy and thus is symbolically free from the tainted inheritance that has been passed down through the Trask generations.

PART FOUR, CHAPTERS 51–55

SUMMARY: CHAPTER 51

> Adam asked, "Do you know where your brother is?"
> "No, I don't," said Cal....
> "He hasn't been home for two nights. Where is he?"
> "How do I know?" said Cal. "Am I supposed to look after him?"
>
> (See QUOTATIONS, p. 61)

Horace Quinn, who has been promoted to sheriff, tells Adam about Cathy's death. Adam weeps and wants to hide Cathy's will from Aron. The sheriff convinces Adam to tell Aron, but no one seems to know where Aron is. When Adam asks Cal about Aron's whereabouts, Cal snarls and asks, "Am I supposed to look after him?" Adam is overcome with a numb shock.

Lee looks through a copy of Marcus Aurelius's *Meditations* and remembers that long ago he stole the book from Samuel Hamilton, who likely knew Lee stole the book but said nothing. Lee goes to see Cal, who has been drinking heavily to cope with his guilt. Cal also has burned the $15,000 cash that his father rejected. Lee tells Cal that he needs to understand that he is simply a normal, flawed human being rather than an abstract and uncontrollable force of evil. This reminder soothes Cal's spirit. On his way out, Lee finds Adam leaning against the wall as if in shock. In his hand is a postcard from Aron informing his father that he has joined the army.

Summary: Chapter 52

As the war takes a hard turn for American troops in Europe, Adam's health takes a similar turn for the worse. He begins to experience numbness and pain in his hand and obsessively wonders and worries about Aron.

Cal speaks with Abra, who tells him that she no longer loves Aron, as he seems to live in a fantasy world of extreme moral contrasts. Cal tells Abra that Aron now knows the truth about Cathy, and Abra confesses that she learned about Cathy long ago. Abra tells Cal that she has fallen in love with him. Cal claims that he is not worthy of her, but Abra implies that she loves Cal precisely because of the moral struggles he undergoes.

At home, Abra's father has withdrawn into seclusion and refuses to return phone calls from a local judge. Abra knows that her father is not sick, as her mother claims, but she is not sure what is wrong with him. Abra gathers up Aron's love letters and burns them.

Summary: Chapter 53

One day, Adam tells Lee that he believes that the fortune his father, Cyrus, amassed was stolen from the Army. Lee contemplates the irony: the honest Adam Trask living his life on a stolen fortune, just as the good Aron Trask might live his life on a fortune made through prostitution.

Abra visits Lee, who is thrilled to see her and says that he wishes he were her father. Abra and Cal talk about the military and agree that Cal is not well suited to life as a soldier. Cal decides to take flowers to Cathy's grave.

Summary: Chapter 54

Adam slowly starts to regain his health. When spring comes, Cal and Abra have a picnic in an azalea grove, where Abra takes Cal's hand and tells him that he must never feel guilty about anything—not even about Aron. Lee looks through a seed catalogue and thinks of the garden he will plant in the spring.

A man comes to the door with a telegram announcing that Aron has been killed in the war. Lee, cursing Aron as a coward, enters Adam's room to tell him the news of his son's death.

SUMMARY: CHAPTER 55
Adam has a stroke upon hearing the news and lies near death when Cal returns to the house. When Lee tells Cal what has happened, the boy is sick with grief and guilt. Cal goes to Abra, who does her best to comfort him. She takes him back to his house, where Lee tells Cal and Abra emphatically that they must always remember that they are in control of their lives and that they are not automatically doomed to repeat their parents' mistakes.

Lee takes Cal and Abra to see the dying Adam. Lee tells Adam that Cal, in informing Aron about his mother, committed a grave sin out of hurt he felt when he believed that Adam did not love him. Lee asks Adam to bless Cal before he dies. As Cal gazes down at him, Adam, with great effort, mouths the single word *timshel,* and then his eyes close in sleep.

ANALYSIS: CHAPTERS 51–55
In the final chapters of the novel, the turnarounds that Cal and Aron experience become complete, as Cal embraces the idea of *timshel* and Aron finalizes his withdrawal from the world by enlisting in the Army. Lee, who is so often the voice of sense and reason in the novel, cements Aron's estrangement from us and from the other characters when he calls Aron a "coward" upon learning of his death. By calling the upright Aron a coward, Lee indicates that he thinks the same way that Abra does—namely, that Aron has retreated into a fantasy world to avoid dealing with the hard moral choices and temptations of the world.

Aron's death completes the Cain-Abel story for Cal and Aron and leaves Cal in a misery of guilt and self-recrimination. Lee, however, advises Cal with a message of sense and optimism, saying that Cal should remember that he is simply a flawed human being, not a monster of evil like his mother. By giving this advice, Lee gently works to undermine the sense of moral determinism that has pervaded the novel and the Trask family since the start—the idea that people are doomed to act out the characteristics with which they are born. Lee's advice to Cal provides a load-lightening affirmation that *timshel,* the freedom to choose between good and evil, really exists.

Adam's final blessing of Cal represents a supreme moment of redemption both for Cal, who can now move beyond his guilt into a happier life with Abra, and for Adam, who makes up for the hurt he has caused Cal by preferring Aron. With Cathy and Aron gone, moral extremism—toward evil in Cathy's case, toward good in Aron's case—no longer dominates the Trask family. Rather than having a choice between only two extreme paths, Cal now has the freedom to resolve his inner moral conflict by taking a middle road. The optimism of the novel's conclusion—as spring approaches and Lee plans to plant a garden—leads us to believe that Cal at last fully understands what *timshel* means and that he can overcome the agony of the past. Just as Cain kills Abel in the Bible, Cal commits sin and indirectly causes Aron's death—but this time, with his father's blessing, Cain confronts the sins of his fathers and is redeemed.

IMPORTANT QUOTATIONS EXPLAINED

1. I believe there are monsters born in the world to human
    parents. Some you can see, misshapen and horrible, with
    huge heads or tiny bodies. . . . And just as there are physical
    monsters, can there not be mental or psychic monsters
    born? The face and body may be perfect, but if a twisted
    gene or a malformed egg can produce physical monsters,
    may not the same process produce a malformed soul?

The narrator uses these words to introduce Cathy Ames in Chapter
8 of the novel. Throughout the novel, Cathy displays an evil that is
so thorough that it borders on implausible, and the narrator makes
several attempts to explain and understand Cathy's existence. He
hypothesizes that although Cathy is physically beautiful, she is a
"psychic monster," a being with a mental deformity analogous to
others' external, physical deformities. Later in the novel, the narrator revises his opinion of Cathy and wonders whether he was right
in calling her a monster. He seems to become somewhat more sym-
pathetic toward Cathy, musing that "since we cannot know what
she wanted, we will never know whether or not she got it." Indeed,
Cathy's motivations remain a mystery throughout *East of Eden,* as
her schemes seem to have no concrete goal or aim—a problem that
critics have singled out in their writings on Steinbeck's novel.

2. And this I believe: that the free, exploring mind of the
    individual human is the most valuable thing in the world.
    And this I would fight for: the freedom of the mind to take
    any direction it wishes, undirected.

Here, in Chapter 13, in another aside to the story, the narrator sets
for his belief that the power of free will in the human mind is the
most precious of human capabilities. He declares his intention to
fight against any force—ideological, religious, political, or otherwise—that threatens to hinder or constrain this freedom of the individual. In highlighting the importance of free choice early in the
novel, the narrator foreshadows the idea of *timshel,* or freedom to

choose between good and evil, that becomes the main idea in *East of Eden*. Although Cal and other characters struggle with the problem of evil throughout the rest of the novel, the narrator plants a seed of hope early, in these words.

3. "Don't you see? . . . The American Standard translation *orders* men to triumph over sin, and you call sin ignorance. The King James translation makes a promise in 'Thou shalt,' meaning that men will surely triumph over sin. But the Hebrew word, the word *timshel*—'Thou mayest'—that gives a choice. It might be the most important word in the world. That says the way is open."

Lee says these words during his discussion of the Cain and Abel story with Samuel and Adam in Chapter 24. He has just revealed to the other men the outcome of the research he did on the meaning of *timshel*, the word that God utters to Cain when exiling him to the lands east of Eden. According to one translation of the Bible, God *orders* Cain to triumph over sin, while according to another, God *promises* Cain that he will defeat sin. Lee's research, however, has revealed that *timshel* means "thou mayest," implying that God tells Cain that he has a *choice* whether or not to overcome sin. Lee sees this idea of free choice over evil a token of optimism that is central to the human condition. He attempts to convince Adam and Cal of the validity of *timshel* and ultimately succeeds, as Adam gives Cal his blessing and Cal realizes he himself has the power to overcome his family's legacy of evil.

4. I believe that there is one story in the world, and only one. . . . Humans are caught—in their lives, in their thoughts, in their hungers and ambitions, in their avarice and cruelty, and in their kindness and generosity too—in a net of good and evil. . . . There is no other story. A man, after he has brushed off the dust and chips of his life, will have left only the hard, clean questions: Was it good or was it evil? Have I done well—or ill?

In Chapter 34 of *East of Eden*, the narrator discusses his view that the one central narrative in human history is the endless struggle between good and evil. He believes that this recurring conflict is so important to human history that there essentially "is no other story." Each individual, regardless of what his or her ancestors have learned, struggles with the same fundamental problem of evil. In this way, no progress is made as generations pass, for each individual faces the same ancient struggle and the same ancient choices. Although the narrator's idea is somewhat optimistic in that it implies that each individual has free will to reject evil, it also implies that the struggle with evil is endless and inescapable and will therefore always be a part of the human condition.

5. Adam asked, "Do you know where your brother is?"
    "No, I don't," said Cal. . . .
    "He hasn't been home for two nights. Where is he?"
    "How do I know?" said Cal. "Am I supposed to look after him?"

This exchange between Adam and Cal, which appears in Chapter 51, is a direct parallel with the exchange between God and Cain that appears in the book of Genesis in the Bible. After Cain murders Abel, God realizes that Abel is missing and asks Cain where Abel is. Cain retorts, "I know not; am I my brother's keeper?" Adam and Cal's reenactment of this conversation links them explicitly to the biblical story and cements Cal and Aron, respectively, as surrogates for Cain and Abel. There are differences between the two stories, however: whereas Cain murders Abel, Cal causes Aron's death only indirectly. Likewise, whereas Cain is banished for his crime, Cal encounters forgiveness and redemption in his father's blessing at the end of *East of Eden*. In this way, Cal, though a Cain figure, overturns the biblical story and, in the end, demonstrates that he has the power to choose good.

KEY FACTS

FULL TITLE
East of Eden

AUTHOR
John Steinbeck

TYPE OF WORK
Novel

GENRE
Allegorical novel; epic

LANGUAGE
English

TIME AND PLACE WRITTEN
January–November 1951; New York City, Nantucket

DATE OF FIRST PUBLICATION
1952

PUBLISHER
Viking

NARRATOR
The story is told by a third-person narrator who is not omniscient and who greatly resembles John Steinbeck himself. In this sense, the narrator may or may not be a direct mouthpiece for the author. In addition to conveying the events of the novel, the narrator provides commentary and interrupts the story frequently to discuss human history and the human condition more broadly.

POINT OF VIEW
The narrator speaks in the third person and shifts viewpoints among various characters, including Adam Trask, Cal Trask, Samuel Hamilton, Cathy Ames, Joe Valery, and others. The narrator's authorial intrusions into the story often include musings in the first person.

TONE
Philosophical; foreboding; nostalgic; hopeful

TENSE

Past

SETTING (TIME)

1862–1918

SETTING (PLACE)

The Salinas Valley in northern California, with several episodes in Connecticut and Massachusetts

PROTAGONISTS

Adam Trask; Cal Trask

MAJOR CONFLICT

Aware of the legacy of evil that he has inherited from his mother, Cal Trask struggles with the question of whether he is destined to be evil himself or whether he can overcome this evil by free choice.

RISING ACTION

While his sons are still boys, Cyrus Trask works as an army administrator and amasses a fortune, probably through embezzlement. Cathy Ames arrives on the Trasks' doorstep, and Adam falls in love with her and marries her. Adam and Cathy then move to the California, where Adam meets Samuel Hamilton and Cathy unsuccessfully attempts to abort her unborn children. Cathy gives birth to Aron and Cal and promptly deserts the family. The crushed Adam does not know Cathy's fate until Samuel reveals one day that Cathy is working at a nearby brothel. Although the revelation hurts Adam, he eventually confronts Cathy, recognizes her evil, and rejects her. Later, Cal too finds out about his mother's profession. He struggles with this knowledge but keeps it from the fragile Aron. When Cathy confronts Cal one day, he stands up to her attempts at intimidation. The increasingly withdrawn Aron, meanwhile, retreats into the shelter of the church.

CLIMAX

Cal, enraged and jealous when his father rejects Cal's gift of $15,000, takes out his anger on Aron by telling him about their mother's life as a prostitute. Cal then takes Aron to see Cathy at her brothel, fully aware that the revelation will destroy Aron.

KEY FACTS

FALLING ACTION

Shocked by the revelation about his mother, Aron enlists in the army, while Cal gradually wins the love of Abra Bacon. Aron is killed in World War I, and Adam, on his deathbed, finally gives his blessing to Cal.

THEMES

The perpetual contest between good and evil; the freedom to overcome evil; the pain of paternal rejection

MOTIFS

The story of Cain and Abel; fortunes and inheritances

SYMBOLS

The Salinas Valley; Charles's scar

FORESHADOWING

The names of characters foreshadow the roles they play in reenacting the biblical story of Cain and Abel; the narrator's introduction of Cathy as a "monster" foreshadows her numerous evil deeds; the narrator's musings on the importance of the individual in shaping human history foreshadow the idea of *timshel* and the ultimately hopeful message of the novel; Samuel's mention that the biblical Aaron did not make it to the Promised Land foreshadows Aron's death.

STUDY QUESTIONS & ESSAY TOPICS

STUDY QUESTIONS

1.   *What symbolic roles do wealth and inheritance play in the novel? How is Adam able to sidestep the moral taint of Cyrus's fortune? How is Cal able to do so?*

There are three large inheritances in the Trask family in *East of Eden*, each worth about $100,000: Cyrus's fortune, which he splits between Adam and Charles; Charles's fortune, which he splits between Adam and Cathy; and Cathy's fortune, which she gives solely to Aron. Each fortune is made up of part of the fortune before it: Cyrus's fortune is the core of Charles's, Charles's the core of Cathy's. All of this money is ill-gotten—earned through theft, blackmail, bad faith, and prostitution. In this light, it symbolizes the biblical idea of original sin, the inherently human evil that is passed down through the generations. Cyrus's evil afflicts Charles, and Charles's evil afflicts Cathy. Aron's psychological breakdown when he realizes the truth about his mother largely stems from his worry about this idea of inherited sin. Aron fears that Cathy's evil makes him inherently evil, and this fear is what shatters him. When Cathy leaves her entire fortune to Aron upon her death, an enormous symbolic burden is placed on his shoulders. Adam effectively sidesteps the taint of inheritance by losing the money in a poorly executed business venture. Ultimately, Steinbeck rejects the idea of inherited moral determinism by replacing it with the idea of *timshel,* that each individual is free to choose his own moral destiny. Because Cal is the character who finally comes to embody the idea of *timshel,* it is appropriate that he should not inherit a cent of Cathy's fortune.

2.   *What role does the story of Cain and Abel play in* East
      of Eden? *What is the significance of the novel's title?*

The biblical story of Cain and Abel, the sons of Adam and Eve, provides the narrative framework of Steinbeck's novel. In the Bible,
Cain, jealous that God approves of Abel's sacrificial offering over
Cain's, kills Abel and then lies to God about it. *East of Eden*
explores the fundamental conflict of good and evil in human life and
essentially retells the story of Cain and Abel twice, once with Adam
and Charles and once with Aron and Cal. The latter is the more
direct retelling, as Cal's revelation of the truth about their mother to
Aron indirectly causes Aron's death. Furthermore, when Adam asks
Cal where Aron has gone, Cal's snarling response—"Am I supposed
to look out for him?"—mirrors Cain's famous retort to God, "Am I
my brother's keeper?"

    A discrepancy between two different translated versions of the
story of Cain and Abel illuminates the idea of *timshel,* the notion
that each individual is free to choose his or her own moral path.
Timshel becomes the central thematic idea in *East of Eden,* as it
enables Cal and Adam to be redeemed from guilt for Aron's death.
The Cain and Abel story also gives the novel its title: after disobey-
ing God, Cain is exiled to the land of Nod, which lies "on the east of
Eden." Additionally, the title implies that the novel's characters, like
the first biblical family, have been expelled from moral paradise and
are forced to contend with the world of human evil and sin, embod-
ied by Cathy.

3. *What role does Lee play in the novel? How would you characterize Steinbeck's portrayal of him?*

Though he may initially appear to be merely a secondary character, Lee is one of the most important figures in the novel. Despite his humorous introduction—of Chinese origin and American birth, he mimics a Chinese accent to play into the expectations of white Americans, outsmarting them all the while—Lee ultimately becomes the voice of wisdom and reason in the novel and often articulates some of the novel's most important themes. It is Lee who researches and explains the idea of *timshel* and discovers the true meaning of the word. Furthermore, it is Lee who reassures Cal that he is a normal, flawed human being, not a monstrous force of evil simply because his mother, Cathy, is evil. Throughout the novel, Lee proves to be a subtle, intelligent man who continually thwarts the expectations both we and the other characters hold for him. Acting as a force of stability and constancy within the Trask household, Lee exposes the racial prejudices of some of the other characters—the deputy who calls him "Ching Chong," for instance—in their ridiculousness and irrelevance.

SUGGESTED ESSAY TOPICS

1. *Although Steinbeck portrays Cathy as a near-inhuman creature of seemingly inherent evil, the idea of* timshel *implies that she has the power to choose her own path. Is Cathy born a moral monster, or does she become one of her own accord? What elements of Cathy's character or episodes from the novel lead you to your conclusion?*

2. *What symbolic values do characters' names hold in* EAST OF EDEN? *Discuss specifically the role of biblical names and the importance of the letters A and C.*

3. *What role do the Hamiltons play in the novel, given that the Steinbeck explores most of his moral concerns through his portrayal of the Trask family? What is the significance of the fact that the narrator is descended from the Hamiltons?*

4. *Is there any difference between the narrator of* EAST OF EDEN *and Steinbeck himself, or is the narrative voice essentially Steinbeck's own? How does this affect your reading of the novel?*

5. *There are several secondary echoes of the Cain and Abel story apart from the obvious parallels with Charles and Adam, Cal and Aron. What are some of these echoes, and what is their role in the novel? (Think about, for example, Dessie Hamilton's death and Abra's reaction to her father's corruption.)*

Review & Resources

Quiz

1. In what eastern state is the original Trask farm located?

   A. Massachusetts
   B. Connecticut
   C. Maryland
   D. Virginia

2. What does the young Adam give his father as a birthday gift?

   A. A saddle
   B. A puppy
   C. A knife
   D. A copy of the Bible

3. To what U.S. government post is Cyrus appointed?

   A. Secretary of the Treasury
   B. Attorney General
   C. Secretary of the Army
   D. Secretary of State

4. In the Bible, Cain and Abel are the sons of whom?

   A. Abraham and Sarah
   B. Adam and Eve
   C. Jacob and Leah
   D. Isaac and Rebekah

5. In which region of California does most of *East of Eden* take place?

   A. The San Fernando Valley
   B. The San Joaquin Valley
   C. The Salinas Valley
   D. The Owens Valley

6. How does Cathy kill her parents?

    A. She burns down their house
    B. She poisons them
    C. She shoots them
    D. She drowns them

7. How does Charles react when he learns that Adam and Cathy have married?

    A. He is overjoyed
    B. He is jealous
    C. He is disgusted
    D. He is indifferent

8. What does Cathy do when Samuel tries to help her deliver her babies?

    A. She thanks him
    B. She passes out
    C. She asks him to fetch Liza instead
    D. She bites him

9. What puzzles Lee about the story of Cain and Abel in the Bible?

    A. He does not understand Cain's motivation for killing Abel
    B. There is a discrepancy between two different translations of the story
    C. He wonders why God punishes Cain so harshly
    D. He is curious where the garden of Eden might have been located

10. What type of business does Faye run?

    A. A saloon
    B. A gambling house
    C. A cabaret
    D. A brothel

11. According to Lee, what does the Hebrew word *timshel* mean?

    A. "Thou shalt"
    B. "Do thou"
    C. "Thou mayest"
    D. "Thou art not"

12. Who is Cotton Eye?

    A. The local sheriff's deputy in Salinas
    B. The piano player at Faye's
    C. An ex-convict who blackmails Cathy
    D. Cathy's pimp

13. According to the original biblical story, what motivates Cain to kill Abel?

    A. Greed
    B. Ambition
    C. Jealousy
    D. Nothing; Cain kills Abel by mistake

14. Which of the Hamilton brothers commits suicide over guilt about Dessie's death?

    A. George
    B. Will
    C. Tom
    D. Joe

15. What, according to the narrator, is the one recurring story in human history?

    A. The conflict among the generations
    B. The struggle between good and evil
    C. The search for the meaning of life
    D. The struggle of the poor

REVIEW & RESOURCES

16. In what kind of business does Adam lose his fortune?

    A. Mining
    B. Cattle
    C. Construction
    D. Refrigeration

17. Which daughter's death crushes Samuel?

    A. Dessie's
    B. Lizzie's
    C. Olive's
    D. Una's

18. Where does Aron go to college?

    A. Stanford
    B. Berkeley
    C. Harvard
    D. Dartmouth

19. What type of store does Lee wish to open in San Francisco?

    A. A clothing store
    B. A bookstore
    C. A restaurant
    D. A grocery

20. What does Cal ultimately do with the $15,000 that was meant to be a gift to his father?

    A. He keeps it
    B. He gives it to charity
    C. He uses it to start a business
    D. He burns it

21. Toward the end of the novel, what does Cathy wear around her neck?

    A. A locket containing Aron's picture
    B. A string of black pearls
    C. A red velvet ribbon
    D. A vial filled with grains of morphine

22. To whom does Cathy leave all her wealth when she dies?

   A.   Aron
   B.   Cal
   C.   Adam
   D.   Charles

23. Why does Aron join the Army?

   A.   Out of a patriotic desire to serve his country
   B.   Out of horror at learning his mother's identity
   C.   Because his father wants him to
   D.   Because he cannot find any other job

24. In what war is Aron killed?

   A.   The Civil War
   B.   The Spanish-American War
   C.   World War I
   D.   World War II

25. Which character was Steinbeck's mother in real life?

   A.   Cathy Ames
   B.   Abra Bacon
   C.   Dessie Hamilton
   D.   Olive Hamilton

ANSWER KEY:

1: B; 2: B; 3: C; 4: B; 5: C; 6: A; 7: C; 8: D; 9: B; 10: D; 11: D; 12: B; 13: C; 14: C; 15: B; 16: D; 17: D; 18: A; 19: B; 20: C; 21: D; 22: A; 23: B; 24: C; 25: D

REVIEW & RESOURCES

SUGGESTIONS FOR FURTHER READING

BENSON, JACKSON J. *John Steinbeck, Writer: A Biography.* New York: Penguin USA, 1990.

FENSCH, THOMAS, ed. *Conversations with John Steinbeck.* Jackson: University Press of Mississippi, 1988.

GEORGE, STEPHEN K., ed. *John Steinbeck: A Centennial Tribute.* Westport, Connecticut: Praeger Publishers, 2002.

STEINBECK, ELAINE, and ROBERT WALLSTEN, eds. *Steinbeck: A Life in Letters.* New York: Penguin USA, 1989.

STEINBECK, JOHN. *Journal of a Novel: The* East of Eden *Letters.* New York: Penguin USA, 1990.

———. *To a God Unknown.* New York: Penguin Classics, 1933.

———. *Of Mice and Men.* New York: Penguin Classics, 1937.

———. *The Long Valley.* New York: Penguin Classics, 1938.

———. *The Grapes of Wrath.* New York: Penguin Classics, 1939.